A Bag of Scraps

Quilts and the Garment District

Edie McGinnis

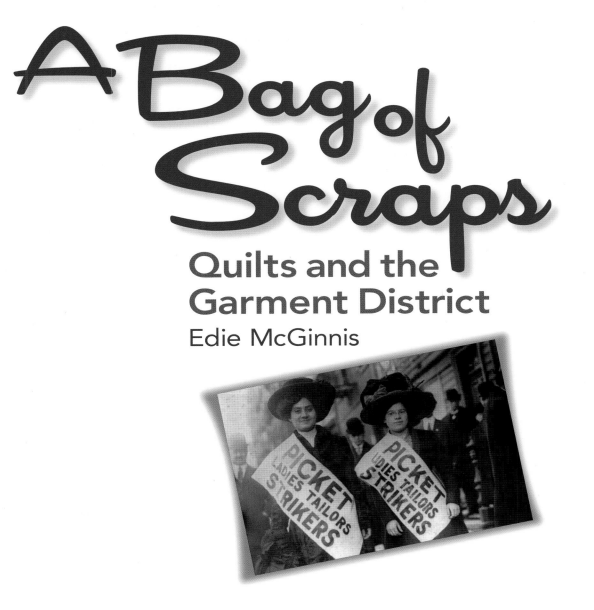

A Bag of Scraps
Quilts and the Garment District
By Edie McGinnis

Editor: Deb Rowden
Designer: Amy Robertson
Photography: Aaron T. Leimkuehler
Illustration: Eric Sears
Technical Editor: Jane Miller
Production assistance: Jo Ann Groves

Published by:
Kansas City Star Books
1729 Grand Blvd.
Kansas City, Missouri, USA 64108

First edition, first printing
ISBN: 978-1-61169-041-5

Library of Congress Control Number: 2012933895

Printed in the United States of America by Walsworth
Publishing Co., Marceline, MO

To order copies, call StarInfo at (816) 234-4636
and say "Books."

**Photo credits for historical photos
on cover and title page:**
Cover: Ladies sit at their sewing machines during
their work day at the Mary Dean Frocks company
on Eighth Street. Courtesy of The Kansas City Star.
Title page: Two women walk the picket line in New
York, 1910. LC-USZ62-49516 - Library of Congress
Prints and Photographs Division Washington, D.C.
20540 USA.
This page: 10th and Broadway (see page 67).
Missouri Valley Special Collections, Kansas
City Public Library, Kansas City, Missouri.

Contents

Acknowledgements

This is the most frightening part of a book to write. I am always so worried that I will fail to thank someone who has richly earned appreciation. One cannot do a book alone and without the following people this book would never have come to fruition.

Klonda Holt, Jane Kennedy and Cheri Raybourn – thank you so much for your help with sewing. You will find the stunning Starry Path quilt using Cherrywood hand-dyed fabrics that Klonda made on page 52.

Brenda Butcher – her quilting skills add beauty and dimension to the quilts. Her talents extend far and away beyond quilting. Take a peek at the yoyo trinket box on page 90. That was her idea and creation.

My team at The Kansas City Star

Aaron Leimkuehler – Photographer extraordinaire – the best! His attention to detail and his patience are unequaled.

Eric Sears – Artist – Eric is the talented person who drew all the diagrams and templates for this book. He seems to have an innate understanding of exactly what is needed even when I'm stuttering and stammering.

Jo Ann Groves – Jo Ann is the person who imaged the photos for this book. It's no easy task to have the photos match the color in the quilts.

Amy Robertson – Page designer – We supply Amy with the photos and art. She supplies the talent and ingenuity to turn all the parts into a beautiful, readable book.

Jane Miller – Technical editor – Jane is the person everyone wants on the team when it comes to making sure the math is correct. She's a wiz when it comes to making sure directions, fabric yardage and templates are accurate.

Deb Rowden – Editor – clears up my sometimes muddled thoughts and keeps me on task. (I'm afraid that working with me could be a lot like trying to herd cats.)

Doug Weaver and Diane McLendon – they said, "Yes" when I came up with the idea for this book and let me know that they believed in it.

Lissa Alexander – Moda Fabrics – Thank you Lissa for sending me the Blueberry Crumb Cake fabric collection by Blackbird Designs for Moda I used to make the Petticoat Lane Table Topper on page 92. Many of the fabrics used in I Dropped My Little Basket were from the Hometown Collection designed by Sweetwater for Moda.

Ann Brownfield and Harvey Fried – Kansas City Garment District Museum. Thanks for sharing your knowledge and stories about the fashion business in Kansas City. Allowing us to photograph items there and share them with quilters adds dimension to this book.

Marla Day – Senior Curator of K-State's Historic Costume and Textile Museum – thank you for pulling out all those quilts so I could look for quilts that might meet the requirements of using scraps from the garment districts. She is a fountain of information on Nelly Don fashions.

Gloria Nixon – Quilt Historian – Gloria made this book much richer by sharing her Red-E-Kut quilt kits and allowing us to photograph them for this book. She also gave me some clues on finding information to help me prove my point. What a dear friend she is!

Thank you, one and all!
—*Edie McGinnis*

About the Author

Edie McGinnis, Kansas City Star author and editor, began her career with The Star in 1987. She recently retired after nearly 21 years with the company. Edie continues to work on a part-time basis as a consultant, editor and author for The Kansas City Star. She contributes as a columnist on The Star's website Pickledish.com and has had several single patterns published. She has written and had published over a dozen quilt books. In 2010, Edie and Jan Patek teamed up and designed the Block of the Month series, Across the Wide Missouri, which ran in The Kansas City Star.

Edie gives lectures and trunk shows on The Kansas City Star quilt patterns, their history and the designers who worked at The Star in the early years; Feedsacks; and using precuts. She has taught quilting at Primitives of the Midwest in Lee's Summit, Missouri, and various workshops using her own original patterns. She has been quilting for more than 35 years and is a member of the American Quilting Society.

The Poindexter building on the corner of 8th and Broadway, home to The Kansas City Garment District Museum. A portion of the proceeds from this book will go to support Kansas City's Garment District Museum.

Dresden Plate Quilt
Kit packets and block
from the Red-E-Kut Quilt Patch
Company. Many of the pieces had the
same print but were different color ways.

Introduction

A chance remark made by a friend—recollections—a photograph—an old quilt top—one never knows what might be the inspiration for a book.

For this book, the inspiration was two-fold. I was driving to Hannibal, Missouri, and had convinced my friend, Klonda Holt, to come along with me. I had been through Hannibal the previous weekend to go to a wedding reception and had stopped at The Hickory Stick (Pat Waelder's wonderful quilt shop) and picked up a few fat quarters of fabric. I was on a quest for yardage this time.

Klonda and I were chatting when she said, "You ought to do a book on Nelly Don." I thought about that for a moment and said, "Maybe not Nelly Don, but the garment district in Kansas City. Maybe they sold scraps by the pound."

The next day I was off and running. Researching on my computer for information was my first step.

What? What's this? We have a Garment District Museum right here in Kansas City? How could I have missed this! My friend Alma Allen and I went for a visit. They have manikins dressed in garments that had been produced by different factories in the district. Some wore Nelly Don fashions, one guy sported a powder blue leisure suit, and a fancy outfit of hot pants from the 1970s hung from a hanger.

Ah, and the maternity outfits that are, thankfully, no longer produced. Did you know in years past there was a hole in the skirt for that baby bump? The only things that kept the skirt on a woman's body were ties. The blouse hung long to cover up the hole in the skirt. It wasn't until the late '50s or early '60s that garment makers added a stretchy panel to cover a woman's stomach.

I discovered that K-State in Manhattan, Kansas, has a Historic Costume and Textile Museum. I made an appointment to see what I could find out about quilts and the garment district. One of the most important things I discovered was that for garment district information, I needed to go back to the source: Kansas City.

As I was thinking about quilts to put in this book, I thought about a fan quilt I made in 1994. My stepmother, Mary, had given me three quilt tops. One of them looked pretty ho-hum at first glance. Maybe it was supposed to be a sunflower quilt and it hadn't been finished. But as it stood, it was put together like a Dresden Plate with a very large hole for the center. The circles had been appliquéd onto white muslin squares and many of the pieces faded into the background.

The pieces that made up the circles were intriguing though. There were plaids included: I kept finding the same plaid again and again but in different color ways. No woman I know buys fabric like that. The plaid wasn't the only fabric I found in different colors, there were at least five different pieces like that.

My sister, Shari, was there when Mary gave me the quilt tops. The next day we went to Peg and Lil's quilt shop in Washington, Illinois. We took the quilt tops along and showed them to Peggy McFeeters. She carefully went over the quilt and said she was fairly certain the pieces had come from the Princess Peggy Dress Factory in Peoria, Illinois.

The fabric choices suddenly made sense. If one had bought remnants or a bag of scraps from a dress factory, one could have a quilt that reflected the dress fabrics in every different color option available.

Quilts, dress scraps, I think I might be on to something here. Go ahead, turn the page and come along with me on my quest.

A large crowd of newly arrived immigrants gathered outside of the main building on Ellis Island. LC-USZ62-40105 Library of Congress Prints and Photographs Division Washington, D.C. 20540 USA http://hdl.loc.gov/loc.pnp/pp.print

A Bag of Scraps

Give me your tired, your poor,
Your huddled masses yearning to breathe free,
The wretched refuse of your teeming shore,
Send these, the homeless, tempest tossed,
I lift my lamp beside the golden door.

—EMMA LAZARUS

So read the most famous lines of the inscription engraved on a plaque mounted on the inside of the pedestal of the Statue of Liberty. There stands the lady with her torch held high as she welcomes immigrants searching for a better life in America.

They came, these people from foreign lands trying to escape famine, religious, racial, and political persecution and lack of economic opportunities. How difficult it must have been for them to leave their homes and their families knowing the probability of ever seeing their loved ones again was practically nil. And how heartbreaking for a mother or father to send their daughter or son off to a foreign land. When that child left she or he took the future of the family with him. No grandbabies to cuddle, nothing but letters and the occasional black and white photo.

Garment workers on the East Side, New York. Vincenzie, 14 years old, Jovannina, 9 years old, and Michael, 5 years old. LC-DIG-nclc-04082 Library of Congress Prints and Photographs Division, Washington, D.C.

By the time the early 1900s rolled around, the majority of the people coming to the United States were from Eastern and Southern Europe. They tended to congregate according to trades they already knew. Some flocked to the coal mines or steel mills, some to the textile mills, some plied their needlework skills.

While some of the immigrants settled in agricultural areas, the majority settled in larger cities. Even though the living conditions were often dismal at best, there was comfort in numbers. For the new arrival, comfort could be found in the ethnic neighborhoods of a large city. They could speak their own language and be understood. They could find churches where they were familiar with the rituals and feel at home. Neighborhoods eased the feelings of loneliness to those who

A YARD OF PRISCILLA SHIRT

No. 711 No. 712 No. 713 No. 714 No. 715 No. 716 No. 717 No. 718 No. 719

The Modern Priscilla, the Standard Embroidery and Fancy-work Magazine, is authority for all kinds of Art Needlework, Silk Embroidery, and Lace Work, China, Oil, and Water-color Painting. Published monthly. Subscription price, 50 cents a year.

THE MODERN PRISCILLA, 221 COLUMBUS AVEN

Advertisement for sewing patterns by *The Modern Priscilla*, a needlework magazine, showing 16 different designs for shirtwaists, with details about patterns and materials. LC-DIG-ppmsca-09489 - Library of Congress Prints and Photographs Division Washington, D.C. 20540 USA

had left their families behind.

Life was far from easy for a newcomer with little money, family or connections. Factories paid little and working conditions were often hazardous. The housing situation was abominable. Overcrowding and unsanitary conditions were the norm. Often there would be 10 people living in one or two rooms.

It didn't take long for a newcomer to become disillusioned but few gave up and went back home. Instead they

Crowds gather outside of the pier morgue. Triangle Waist Co. fire, N.Y.C. LC-USZ62-91066 Library of Congress Prints and Photographs Division Washington, D.C. 20540 USA

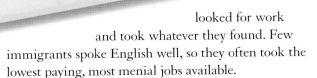

looked for work and took whatever they found. Few immigrants spoke English well, so they often took the lowest paying, most menial jobs available.

Many worked in the sweatshops making garments or even parts of garments. As if putting in the long hours demanded of them wasn't enough, they took work home with them in the evenings just to try to make ends meet. It

was there that whole families became involved in earning a livelihood. Even small children were expected to help.

Triangle Waist Company

New York's Triangle Waist Company was a perfect example of the type of working conditions new immigrants endured.

Nearly 600 people worked at the Triangle Waist Company's factory located on the upper floors of the Asch building in Manhattan. Most were women, if you could call a 13 or 14-year-old girl a woman. They put in some long days and worked six days a week. Every day they turned out the fashionable women's blouses called shirtwaists that had puffy sleeves and a tight waist.

It was nearly closing time that spring Saturday afternoon March 11, 1910. The workers were beginning to gather their belongings together and were probably chattering about plans for their day off much as people do now. "Fire!" The cry went up and panic ensued as the workers tried to escape the flames.

On the ninth floor was a stairwell but the door had been locked, effectively trapping the people inside. This was a common practice by owners who were fearful of having goods stolen from them. The fire escape led nowhere and was so flimsy that it bent under the weight of the people trying to use it. It was the only fire escape in the building.

Some workers went to the windows and saw with horror that the firemen's ladders were at least three stories too short. Not even the water from the hoses could effectively reach the fire. Many jumped to their death rather than being burned alive. Even the firemens' nets failed to hold the bodies that came hurtling out the windows.

In less than 30 minutes it was over. 146 young people were dead, many of them strewn about on the sidewalks.

As the dead were slowly identified and more and more facts came to light, angry voices rose in protest at the senselessness of so many deaths. The locked door, the weak fire escape that went nowhere, the doors that opened in rather than out, the greed of the owners and their lack of concern for the welfare of their employees, all opened the doors for the union to become strong in the garment industry.

Above: Two women walk the picket line in New York, 1910. LC-USZ62-49516 - Library of Congress Prints and Photographs Division Washington, D.C. 20540 USA
Below: Postcard showing the street car tunnel exit used by workers in the garment district. Missouri Valley Special Collections, Kansas City Public Library, Kansas City, Missouri.

Rise of the Union

The unions had their work cut out for them. Inadequate fire protection was rampant among the factories: often hallways and stairwells were so narrow that only one person could get through at a time. Some places had rows of sewing machines blocking the fire escape; some even had the windows barred.

The fire haunted New York and there were changes made in the labor laws and fire codes. Change spread across the country. And while it was well and good to change the laws and fire codes, it benefitted no one if they weren't enforced. The ILGWU made safety and sanitation a large part of the contracts they negotiated for their workers. Workers went on strike to prove they were serious when the union deemed it necessary.

Other Garment Bases

New York may have been home to the most garment manufacturers in the United States but it wasn't the only city with a large business base in the industry. Chicago, St. Louis, Los Angeles, Dallas, Minneapolis and Kansas City all held their own as top producers of clothing.

Kansas City, situated at the junction of the Kansas and the Missouri rivers, was a prime location for industry. As bridges were completed, especially those that would carry trains, Kansas City became a force to reckon with in terms of cost-effective shipping.

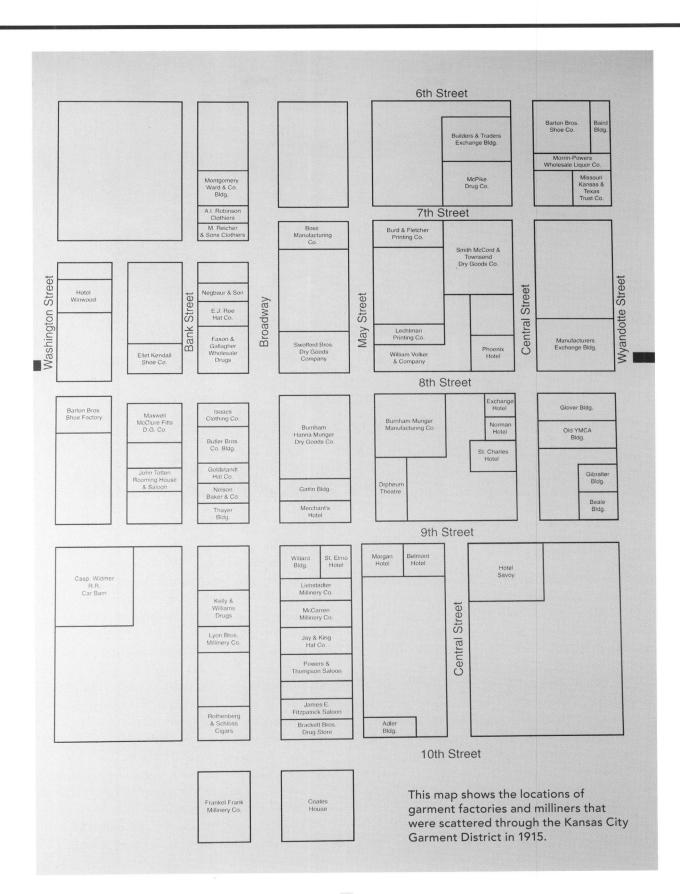

This map shows the locations of garment factories and milliners that were scattered through the Kansas City Garment District in 1915.

Ladies sit at their sewing machines during their work day at the Mary Dean Frocks company on Eighth Street. Courtesy of The Kansas City Star

In the mid-1800s, when Kansas City was still "small town," the area that became known as the garment district was residential. By the time the 1900s rolled around, the area from 6th Street to 11th Street around Broadway had become industrialized and was home to various wholesale dry goods shops and 11 clothing manufacturers.

In its heyday, the garment industry was the second largest employer in Kansas City with over 4,000 people on the payroll. Only the Stockyards employed more people.

Most of the employees lived on the Kansas side of the city. It would have been a tough haul to get to work had it not been for the streetcar tunnel that began on the Kansas Side of the city and ended at the corner of Eighth Street and Washington.

Workers had only a short distance to walk once they left the tunnel (see the photo on page 12).

Assembly Line

Unlike its counterpart in New York, Kansas City did not have a large base of skilled immigrants to draw on; especially those who could make a garment from start to finish. Nell Donnelly Reed is credited by some for introducing an assembly line routine for making garments.

Workers in Kansas City were trained to do one aspect of the job. Some would sew collars or pockets or perhaps, press cuffs for eight hours a day. It sounds like it would be boring as can be but according to this excerpt that ran in The Kansas City Star by Brian Burnes and Tanika White, April 29, 1997, that wasn't necessarily so.

"I was an iron presser, and I liked it," said Marie Strickland, who worked in the district for about 25 years. For eight hours each day she'd press sleeves, cuffs, collars and coats with a heavy steam iron.

"They had big fans in the ceiling and that kept the air circulating, and in the summertime they would raise the windows," said Strickland. "But you'd sweat. When you'd get through, you'd be good and wet from using them irons."

"… Garment work was hard but also delicate. A collar or cuff had to have a certain roll to it.

"You had to run it at a certain angle so you could press it and not have any wrinkles," Strickland said. "It was a skill … It made me feel that I had accomplished something that I could do and do it professionally."

Below, clockwise from top: This machine was used to make buttonholes. Not only did it stitch, it also cut the hole for the button. Bottom right: Typical sewing machine with knee lift used by garment workers. Bottom left: This machine was used for bar-tacking. Bar tacks are made using a tight zigzag stitch and were done on the edge of pockets to keep the fabric from tearing from hard use. Middle left photo: Left, straight cutting knife, right, serging machine.

Mary Dean Frocks

Mary Dean Frocks was located in the Mercantile Exchange building located in the heart of the garment district at 210 West Eighth Street, in Kansas City. Row after row of workers sat at their machines producing their one little section of a garment.

The sewing machines used were industrial strength and, unlike today's home sewing machine, did only one task. They straight-stitched and were efficient. They even had a knee-lift feature so the operator could stop her machine with the needle down and turn the piece without lifting the presser foot by hand. (And you thought that was a new feature!)

There was a machine that made buttonholes and cut them as well. One machine was used

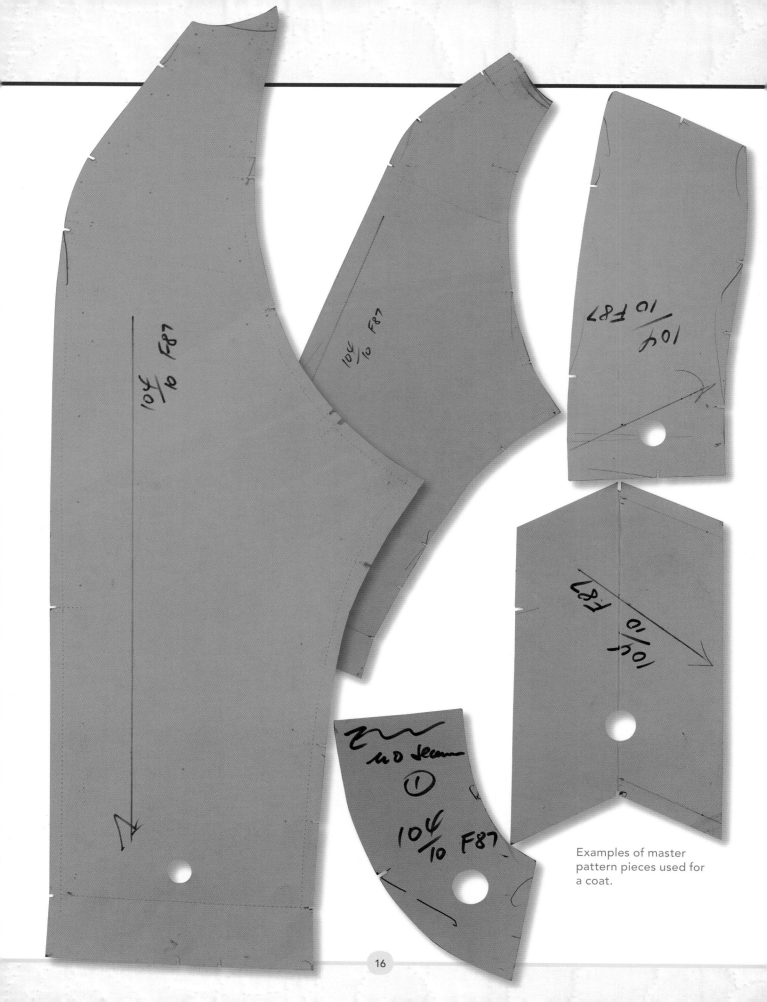

Examples of master pattern pieces used for a coat.

This fashion ad promoted the clothing produced in Kansas City.

when bar-tacking pockets on suits, another for serging. It was no wonder that one became a skilled expert in their field.

The process of actually turning out a garment began with design and a pattern. By the time the pattern had been finalized, a master pattern was cut from lightweight cardboard. It was traced onto gridded, dotted paper leaving as little space between pieces as possible. The paper pattern was then placed onto fabric that had been layered and stacked on a cutting table. The pieces were cut out with a cutting knife then distributed to the machine operators who would sew those particular pieces together.

After the item had been finished, it was inspected and placed on a rack, ready to find it's home in a store, then into a customer's closet.

All kinds of garments were made in Kansas City. Women's coats, suits and dresses; men's work clothes and underwear; girls' dresses and coats; sportswear, uniforms – carried labels from the manufacturers in Kansas City. One of the national fashion ads promoted Kansas City-made fashions by showing a variety of labels. It was said that one in every seven women in the country wore a garment that had been made in Kansas City.

Nell Donnelly Reed

Perhaps the most colorful and well-known woman to step out of the Garment District was Ellen Quinlan Donnelly Reed, better known as Nell Donnelly Reed. She came from Parsons, Kansas, and as the twelfth child of thirteen, was on a first-name basis with hand-me-downs. With a natural bent for stitching and design, she remade the clothing she was given.

She married Paul Donnelly and the pair moved to Kansas City in 1906. She thought the cotton dresses offered to women were ugly and shapeless and did nothing for the woman wearing one. Nell wouldn't have been caught dead wearing one of those Mother Hubbard styles and set to work designing and sewing her own clothing.

Her neighbors were enchanted with Nell's designs and soon she was sewing for her friends. At their urging, she took a sample of her designs to some of the downtown stores in Kansas City and came home with her first order for 18 dozen house dresses from the George B. Peck Dry Goods Company in 1916. While most dresses sold for about 50 cents, Donnelly upped the ante and charged $1.00 for hers.

With start-up money of a mere $1,270, she was off and running. Peck's first order sold out in less than two hours. Donnelly Garment Co. manufactured the line of house dresses under the Nelly Don label and became one of the largest makers of women's wear in the country.

It was Paul Donnelly who provided the start-up cash for the company and he helped lead it to the success it enjoyed. By 1929, the company employed more than 1,000 workers and produced 5,000 dresses per day using the section work assembly line.

But living with Paul Donnelly was no bed of roses. He was unstable, an alcoholic with a bad habit of threatening to kill himself if his wife ever got pregnant and had a child. His wife estimated that she had gotten rid of over 30 guns by sneaking them out of the house or office.

1931 was a tumultuous year for the Donnelly family. Friends and family were told that Nell was taking a trip to Europe to adopt a baby. She did indeed come home with an infant, a little boy she named David. But she had not gone to Europe; her trip had been to Chicago where she stayed until she gave birth to her son, fathered by her lover James A. Reed.

Reed had served two terms as mayor of Kansas City and three-terms as senator. He had also run for president three times. After retiring from the Senate, he practiced law with his partner, James E. Taylor. It was clear that Reed had some clout among the power brokers in Kansas City.

On December 16, 1931, Donnelly and her chauffer, George Blair, were returning to her home on Oak Street about 6 p.m., when they had to stop because a car was blocking the end of the drive. An armed man got into the car beside Blair, tied him up, blindfolded him, and took

Nell Donnelly

over driving the car.

Two other men had entered the car and sat on either side of Donnelly. They made her lie on the floorboard. She was there for nearly an hour, and unable to see anything that was happening.

Donnelly and Blair were taken to a grubby four-room cottage on a farm north of Bonner Springs, Kansas, that had been rented by 29-year-old Paul Scheidt. There Blair was kept blindfolded and trussed up while Nell was forced to lie on a cot under the guard of hoodlum, Charley Mele.

Paul Donnelly received a note the next day that said Blair would be killed and Nell blinded if the kidnappers didn't get $75,000. No police or other authority was to be notified. Donnelly's lawyer, James Taylor, received three notes one of which was written by Nell herself, authorizing him to withdraw the money from her husband's checking account.

After speaking to Paul, Taylor called his partner, James Reed, and apprised him of the situation. Reed was in the midst of arguing a case in Jefferson City when he asked the judge to let him leave. The judge granted him permission and Reed hurried back to Kansas City.

Rumors raced through the courthouse about Reed leaving so quickly. People were fairly certain that something had happened concerning the Donnelly family but they speculated it concerned their newly "adopted" son who was only 14 weeks old.

Once the rumor circulated in Jefferson City that Nell had been kidnapped, the police in Kansas City heard about it and so did The Kansas City Star. The December 17th issue of the evening paper's headline read, "Kidnap 'Nelly Don.'"

Worried that the kidnappers might exact retribution on their captives because of the heavy publicity, Reed stepped forward and sent the kidnappers a message. The Kansas City Star published the following:

"If these men release or deliver Mrs. Donnelly unharmed, they can have their $75,000. They can get it in any form they desire and under any conditions they name. In this I am speaking for Mr. Donnelly and I add my personal guarantee. On the other hand, if a single hair on Mrs. Donnelly's head is harmed, I will and Mr. Donnelly will spend the rest of our lives running the culprits to earth and securing for them the extreme penalty of the law, which in Missouri is death by hanging."

Reed was a man of action used to waiting on no one and took matters into his own hands. He picked up the phone and called the most powerful crime boss in Kansas

From top: One of several ransom notes sent to Reed after he became involved in the kidnapping negotiations. Cottage where Donnelly was held captive. Newspaper headlines that ran in The Kansas City Star after Donnelly was released. Photos courtesy of The Kansas City Star.

In 1973, the Garment District was placed on the National Historic Registry so most of the buildings remain. After years of being left vacant or abandoned, many have been restored and turned into office buildings or lofts.

City, Johnny Lazia, and ordered him to have Donnelly released.

Lazia protested and claimed to have nothing to do with kidnapping. In 1931, it wasn't considered good protocol for criminals to go out on their own and kidnap a prominent member of the community without first having permission from the mob. Lazia launched his own search sending out his men and found the cottage where Nell and Blair were being held. The two were released after being held for 34 hours.

Martin Depew and Walter Werner, two of the kidnappers, were caught in South Africa and sent back to Kansas City. They pleaded guilty and were sentenced to life in prison. One of the kidnappers, Paul Scheidt, was found not guilty by a jury even though he had confessed to having taken part in the kidnapping. Charles Mele was tried and sentenced to 35 years in prison for his part in the doomed affair.

The kidnapping, while it ended well, haunted her and in later years, Nell made sure her son alternated his route to and from school. She frequently changed her schedule so it wasn't so predictable.

Nell and Paul Donnelly divorced in 1932. She bought him out of the company for $1 million.

In December of 1933, she married James A. Reed after a quiet dinner party in her apartment. None of the 20 guests had any inkling the party would be closed with a wedding performed by a judge. It took the attendees a while to recover from the shock before they could offer their congratulations. Nell was 44 and Reed was 72.

While the unions had been successful in organizing nearly every shop in Kansas City, Donnelly's was a different story. She was a businesswoman who was far ahead of her time when it came to employer/employee relations. She provided a nurse at her factory that employees could visit if they were hurt or not feeling well. Employees enjoyed camaraderie at company picnics and Christmas parties. The parties and events thrown for the employees included their families as well.

Donnelly even went so far as to purchase a house near 63rd Street and Swope Park. It served as a clubhouse for the employees and any of them could reserve it. No one was ever bumped from their reservation by a person higher up in the chain of command.

In 1937, the union appropriated $100,000 to organize the Nelly Don factory. But they had not reckoned on her power or the loyalty of her employees. For the next 30 years, the union gave it its best shot but it was not to be. Only after she had died and the company had been sold did the workers accept the union. By then the whole industry in Kansas City was going into a decline and Nelly Don closed in 1978.

Where did they go?

In the 1960s, the fashion world was turned upside down. No more demure little print dresses for ladies, they were traded in for hip-hugger jeans (preferably with bell-bottoms) or a mini-skirt or a micro-skirt if you had really good legs. Throw on a halter top or a peasant blouse and grab a purse made from hemp and you were right in style. I think you could call this "hippie couture."

Factories began relocating in areas where labor was cheaper and that can most likely be translated to non-union. Other competitors from overseas started lobbying for business from the large department stores. Smaller specialty shops started going out of business because of the competition presented by big discount retailers like K-Mart and Walmart.

By 1980, only six garment businesses remained in Kansas City.

In 1973, the Garment District was placed on the National Historic Registry so most of the buildings remain. After years of being left vacant or abandoned, many have been restored and turned into office buildings or lofts. And the place where that street car tunnel spewed out thousands of workers every morning has turned into a lovely little park that boasts a 19-foot tall sculpture of a sewing needle and button.

Poindexter building on the corner of Eighth and Broadway

The park is directly across the street from the Historic Garment District Museum that's on the corner of 8th and Broadway. It was founded in 2002 with the support of Ann Brownfield and Harvey Fried. DST Systems, Inc., a principal landowner in the garment district, offered display space in the Poindexter building. Without the help of DST, the Museum might never have found a home.

Ann Brownfield has quite a resume and is no stranger to the Garment District. She graduated from Stephen's College in Columbia, Missouri. After attending Stephen's, she continued her education at Washington University in St. Louis, Missouri.

Brownfield's first job was designing shoes and later junior fancy dresses, then suits while living in St. Louis.

When she and her husband moved to Kansas City, Brownfield found a job designing sportswear for little girls for Debbie Dare. She also designed clothing for Mendel Silverman (Mendel Dresses), Phillip Zarlinsky and Jack Fox, all noted garment houses in the district.

Before starting her own factory in 1979, Ann worked for Brand & Puritz. There she designed the first pants suit for women when the Chiefs started playing football in Kansas City in 1963. She said, "Everyone wanted to be warm when they sat out there in the stadium."

Her cohort at the Museum is Harvey Fried. He's a dapper gentleman with a quick wit and ready smile. He's right at home in the Garment District too. His father started the Fried-Siegel Company, now owned by Fried. They made wool suits and coats that were distributed under the Styline label.

The image on the quilt package reads:

DRESDEN PLATE NO. 4

This package contains enough Red-E-Kut quilt patches to complete one unit of a quilt. All pieces are accurately cut, of uniform quality material, color-fast and preshrunk. The above cut is given as a guide in the piecing of your quilt. Many attractive quilts can be made by the variation in placing these patterns.

Red-E-Kut Quilt Patch Co.
210 West 8th   Kansas City, Mo.

He is determined to preserve the history of the district and loves nothing better than sharing his knowledge. In 2006, Fried was awarded an Urban Hero Award by the Downtown Council of Kansas City. It's an award given to people who have made downtown Kansas City a better place to live, work and visit.

So what happened to all those scraps?

If the cutter was good, all the scraps were pretty small. They were sold to people called "jobbers" according to Harvey Fried. The "jobber" would pick up the scraps from the barrels and bins and resell them to other manufacturers who needed that type of material for their

Dresden Plate Quilt Kit pieces from the Red-E-Kut Quilt Patch Co. Notice the number of pieces that were of the same print but different color ways.

THE LOVER'S KNOT

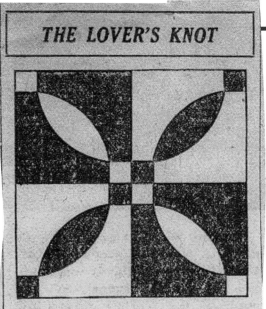

This is an ideal quilt for your hope chest. Just anything isn't suitable for that chest of chests, but this quilt is different. It has "romance" woven into every stitch, and I can just see that brand-new husband displaying it and bragging about what a wonderful needleworker he married. Even tho you have never made a quilt before, you cannot help but make a success of this simple little design with our actual-size piece pattern to guide you. You may obtain the pattern for 15 cents from Quilt Block Service, Capper's Weekly, Topeka, Kan.

Scraps for Quilt Making

So many quilters have written to ask where they may obtain scrap material for quilt-making we have made arrangements with a ready-to-wear women's house dress factory to supply us with left-over scraps. These materials —all colors, all sizes, all shapes, and all washable—have been done up into 2-pound bundles, equal to about 8 yards of material, which we are able to sell at the unusually low price of 75 cents. If you are one of those persons looking for scrap quilting material don't miss one of these bundle bargains. It may be obtained from Quilt Block Service, Capper's Weekly, Topeka, Kan.

Above: This ad for "Mickey" Quilt Patches ran in the *Better Homes and Gardens* December, 1932 issue. Left: Ad from *Capper's Weekly.*

product. Wool scraps usually ended up as roofing material.

But still there were companies that worked with cottons such as Nelly Don and Mary Dean Frocks. Perhaps it's just coincidence but quilt kits marketed under the name Red-E-Kuts bore the same address as Mary

Quilts made from scraps from dress factories usually have more than two color ways of the same print. In some quilts, you will find more than one print repeated.

Dean Frocks. Of course that doesn't prove that they came from that dress factory but still …

Capper's Weekly of Topeka, Kansas, ran an ad answering the question of where a quilter might obtain scrap material for quiltmaking. They said they had made arrangements with a ready-to-wear women's house dress factory to supply them with left-over scraps. One could buy a 2 lb. bundle for 75 cents.

Capper's wasn't the only one advertising those dressmaking scraps for quilters and Red-E-Kuts weren't the only pre-cut quilt kits either. John C. Michael Company from Chicago, Illinois, was also selling them. In an ad advertising "Mickey" Around-the-House Dresses, they said, "We give better value in these dresses because the fabric left over after cutting is used to make the ready-cut patches in our line of quilts. Through this economy we bring you a better garment at a lower price."

"Mickey" quilt patches (page 23) offered Grandmother's Flower Garden quilts with 3,694 cut to size patches complete with instructions. For just a few dollars more, you could order a kit for a Lone Star quilt as well.

According to an article published in *Quilt* magazine 1990 winter edition, written by Elaine Cressionnie, "In all dress factories there are stacks of scraps that fall to the ground when the fabric is stacked up and cut by big machines into the appropriate styles and sizes. The Princess Peggy factory was no exception. They produced mountains of scraps that needed to be disposed of.

"Frequently these fabrics were bagged up and then sold by the pound as scraps for quiltmaking. The bright, happy florals and geometric designs that made the Princess Peggy house dresses so popular were particularly suitable

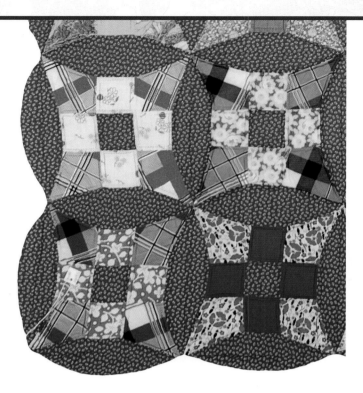

Above: Detail of Improved Nine Patch. Notice the three identical plaid prints grouped together.
Opposite: Improved Nine Patch, 76 x 88 in., ca. 1930. Hand pieced and hand quilted. Historic Costume and Textile Museum, department of apparel, textiles and interior design, Kansas State University, 2010.19.5, gift of Deborah A. Saroff. Photographs by division of communications and marketing.

for quilting." Turn to page 70 to see a quilt made using Princess Peggy Scraps.

What to Look For

As shoppers (and we quilters are shoppers, especially when it comes to fabric), common sense will tell you that we usually do not buy dress fabric that is the same but colored differently. We don't want the same design showing up in our closet even if does come in blue, green, yellow, red or pink. To use the same print defeats the purpose of being original when it comes to sewing, be it garments or quilts.

Quilts made from scraps from dress factories usually have more than two color ways of the same print. In some quilts, you will find more than one print repeated. The

To learn more about the Garment District, see Resources, page 94.

In years to come, I wonder what quilt historians will think of all the quilts made from Jelly Rolls, Layer Cakes, Charm Packs and all the other precuts that are out there. The fabric will most assuredly fit the criteria for quilts made from dress scraps, although the many books about working with these products might give us away.

Red-E-Kut pieces on page 22 show three to five prints in different colors. Since we have the kit(s), it is readily apparent what is going on.

But what if we don't have that kit? Maybe it's best to go back to the common sense train of thought. If we start seeing the same print in multiple color ways (more than two or three), it's probably a safe bet that it came from a bundle of scraps or a kit.

Kansas State University has a textile museum that has a collection of clothing from the Garment District. They also have a nice collection of quilts donated to the University. The curator, Marla Day, and I looked through their quilts hoping to find some that might have been made using factory dress scraps. We are both fairly certain that we were successful.

The first quilt we found that met the criteria of pieces that had the same print in multiple color ways was a Dresden Plate. The prints looked much like the prints in the Red-E-Kut packets.

The second quilt is an improved Nine-Patch (page 25). It was pieced and quilted by hand and the quilter didn't much care about spreading those plaids around. Somehow or another, three of them all ended up in the same corner.

We also found another quilt that we initially thought met the criteria I was using. It is an appliquéd quilt the donor called Morning Glory and was donated to the university by Dorothy Willcoxon. Notice the blue, pink and yellow flowers all have the same print. It can be found in the leaves in green as well.

But this quilt was not made from dress scraps. Rather it was made from a kit sold by the Bucilla Company. According to Merikay Waldvogel, this was kit Number 8099 titled, "Twin Vase." The lid of the kit box has the NRA symbol on it dating it to 1933-1934. Bucilla sold so many kits that they would have ordered the fabric by the bolt.

Alma Irene Hull Cummings of Iowa made a quilt made from the kit, Twin Vase and entered it in the Sears National Quilt Contest during the 1933 World's Fair. It is a match to the Morning Glory quilt owned by the University.

It's difficult to be definitive as to whether or not a quilt was made from scraps from a dress factory unless one has direct provenance. The Red-E-Kut packets are proof. Finding a catalog or advertisement that offers the kit/scraps and promotes it as being cut from ready-to-wear clothing is another clue to be taken into consideration.

Yet another clue indicating the fabric could be scraps from a dress manufacturer is that all the fabric in the quilt is of the same age. If the pieces came from the household scrap bag, there would most likely be fabrics from different eras.

A bag of scraps purchased via mail order would more likely be used for a pieced scrap quilt rather than an appliqué quilt and it would be one of a kind.

In years to come, I wonder what quilt historians will think of all the quilts made from Jelly Rolls, Layer Cakes, Charm Packs and all the other precuts that are out there. The fabric will most assuredly fit the criteria for quilts made from dress scraps, although the many books about working with these products might give us away.

In the following pages you will find scrap quilts, some old, some new, all perfect for using up your own scraps. Enjoy!

Opposite: Morning Glory, 74 x 72 in., ca. 1930. Appliquéd cotton and hand-quilted. Historic Costume and Textile Museum, department of apparel, textiles and interior design, Kansas State University, 2011.13.6, gift of Dorothy Willcoxon. Photographs by division of communications and marketing.

Handy Hints

Templates for Appliqué

I used freezer paper for my appliqué templates on the basket quilt (page 32).

Pin the pieces in place with the shiny side of the freezer paper up and the dull side touching the fabric, then cut them out adding a ⅛" – ¼" seam allowance. Press the seam allowance over the edge of the freezer paper template. An iron heats up the wax on the freezer paper to hold the seam allowance in place and eliminates the need to glue the seam allowances.

If you've prepared your templates as noted above, you will be able to press the pieces in place while checking to see if they are positioned correctly.

Invisible Machine Appliqué

I have a Bernina 440 sewing machine. When I do invisible machine appliqué, I use a blind hem stitch (Stitch No. 7 on my machine). I set the length of the stitch to 1 and the width of the zigzag to 1 as well. I generally use a 50 weight thread that will "sink in" to the fabric rather than changing my thread with every color. For example, a medium brown thread will sink in to red, brown, purple and green fabrics.

Borders

Always measure your quilt through the center horizontally and vertically. After getting that measurement, cut the length of the borders. If you measure on the edge of the quilt, you risk having too much fullness in your borders. For the same reason, it's a bad idea to sew a border on, then trimming it to fit.

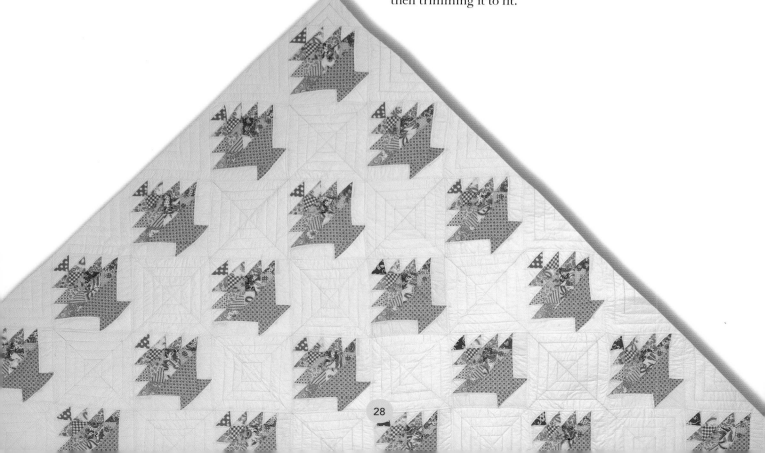

How to Paper Piece

Read this before you begin the Starry Path quilt (page 52). Set up your sewing machine before you begin. Use a 90/14 needle and an open-toe presser foot. Set the stitch length to 18 – 20 stitches per inch. On my machine (a Bernina) that's a 1.5.

Place a small piece of double-sided sticky tape on the blank side of the paper in position 1. The tape will adhere to the paper rather than the fabric. Put your first piece of fabric, right side up, in place. Fold the paper back over the line and trim between position 1 and position 2. Use an Add-A-Quarter ruler to trim the seam allowances in the large blocks and an Add-An-Eighth for small blocks. Butt a piece of template plastic or a note card up to the sewing line when you are folding the paper back.

Line up the edge of the fabric for position 2 with the first piece of fabric, right sides facing. Turn the paper over and stitch on the line between position 1 and position 2. Make sure you sew past the end of each line. Press each piece after it is sewn in place.

Fold the paper back on the line between position 2 and position 3. Butt the Add-A-Quarter ruler up to the paper and trim.

Continue on in this manner until you have all the pieces sewn to the paper. Trim each section along the dotted lines. Do not tear the paper off until all the blocks are complete and sewn together.

Yoyos

Draw around a circle template on the reverse side of the fabric. You'll find the ones used in this book on page 37. Add a ⅛" – ¼" seam allowance when cutting out the circle. Run a basting stitch around the outer edge, turning under the seam allowance as you stitch. The larger the stitches you use, the tighter the gathers in the yoyo will be.

Remove the template and gather the yoyo. Knot off the thread.

Quilts

I Dropped My Little Basket, designed and made by Edie McGinnis, quilted by Brenda Butcher, Independence, Missouri.

I Dropped My Little Basket

Block Size: 6" Finished • Quilt Size: 83" x 91"

Fabric Needed

- 8 yards cream
  (I used a variety of cream fabrics and reserved 3 yards of one for setting triangles, corner triangles and borders.)
- 9 fat quarters of assorted red fabrics
- 1½ yards red for framing border and binding
- 5 fat eighths white on red prints for yoyos
  (By all means, use scraps if you have them on hand. The more variety, the better.)

CUTTING INSTRUCTIONS

Note: templates are on page 37.

From the cream fabric, cut

- 129 – 6½" squares
- 8 – 9¾" squares – Cut each square from corner to corner twice on the diagonal for setting triangles. Set aside. (You will have 2 triangles left over. Save them for another project.)
- 2 – 5⅛" squares – Cut each square from corner to corner once on the diagonal for corner setting triangles. Set aside.
- You will need to cut 6½" strips across the width of the fabric for the outside borders but I recommend waiting until the center of the quilt is complete since there seems to be a lot of variance in our quarter-inch seam allowances.

From the assorted red fabrics, cut

- 129 baskets bases using template A. Add ⅛" – ¼" seam allowance when cutting.
- 129 handles using template B. Add ⅛" – ¼" seam allowance when cutting.
- 8 – 2" strips across the width of the fabric. Set these aside until the center of the quilt is complete.

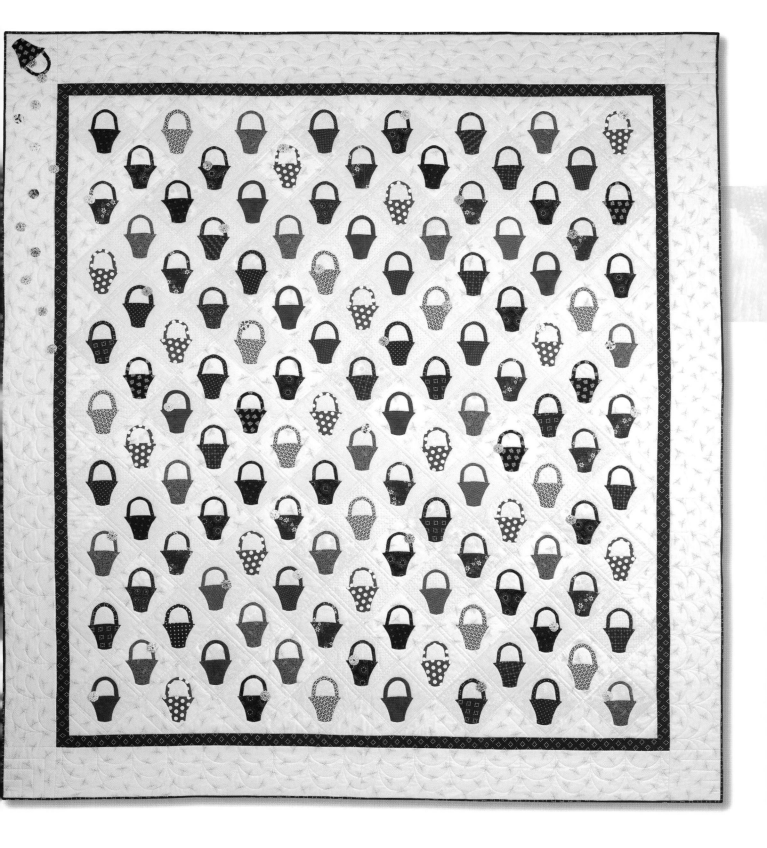

Quilt Assembly

- Prepare the baskets and handles for appliqué using your favorite method. (See "Handy Hints" (page 28) for tips about using freezer paper templates.)

- Stitch the baskets in place onto the background fabric. You will find the placement diagram on page 37. Reserve one basket block for the border. Do not close the top of the border basket completely. You need to leave enough area unsewn to tuck a small yoyo in place.

- After the baskets have been appliquéd in place, arrange the blocks on a design wall. Try not to have 2 baskets using the same fabric next to each other. Refer to the Assembly Diagram.

- Sew the blocks together on the diagonal using a setting triangle at the end of each row where indicated. Press each row as you finish, alternating the direction of the seam allowances.

- Pin and sew the rows together then stitch the corner triangles in place.

- Press the top, then measure it horizontally through the center. Sew 2 – 2" red strips together and trim to your measurement. Make 2 strips like this. Sew one strip to the top of the quilt and one to the bottom. Press the seam allowance toward the red border strip.

- Measure the quilt through the center vertically. Sew 2 – 2" red strips together and trim to your measurement. Make 2. Sew a strip to each side of the quilt top and press the seam allowance toward the red border strip.

- Measure the quilt top again horizontally through the center. Sew 2 – 6½" cream strips together and trim to your measurement. Make 2 strips like this. Sew one strip to the top of the quilt and one to the bottom. Press the seam allowance toward the red border strip.

- Measure the quilt through the center vertically. Sew enough 6½" strips together to equal your measurement. Make 2. Sew one strip to the right side of the quilt top. Press the seam allowance toward the red border strip.

- Sew a basket block onto the end of the remaining 6½" strip and trim the strip to the correct measurement. Refer to the placement diagram for the position of the basket. Sew the border in place and press the seam allowance toward the red border strip.

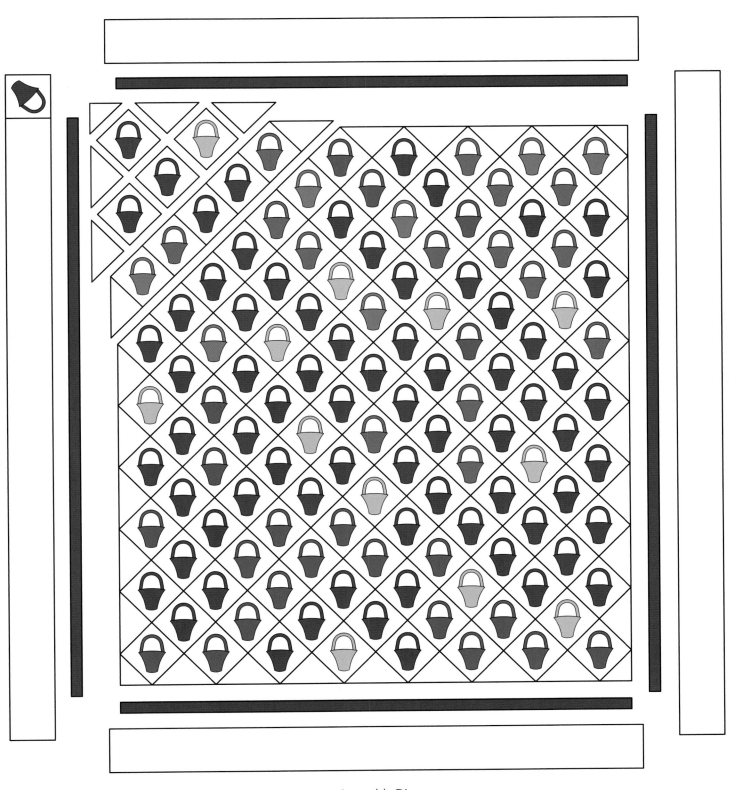

Assembly Diagram

Finishing

- Make 43 – 1¼" yoyos from the red on white prints. You can use one of the new Clover yoyo makers or use the small template on the next page.

- After the quilt has been quilted, stitch the yoyos in place in a random fashion. Spill 12 yoyos down the side border and place others on the basket handles. Refer to the photo for placement purposes.

- Bind the quilt using red bias binding.

Display of Nelly Don items at Kansas City's Garment District Museum located on the corner of 8th and Broadway.

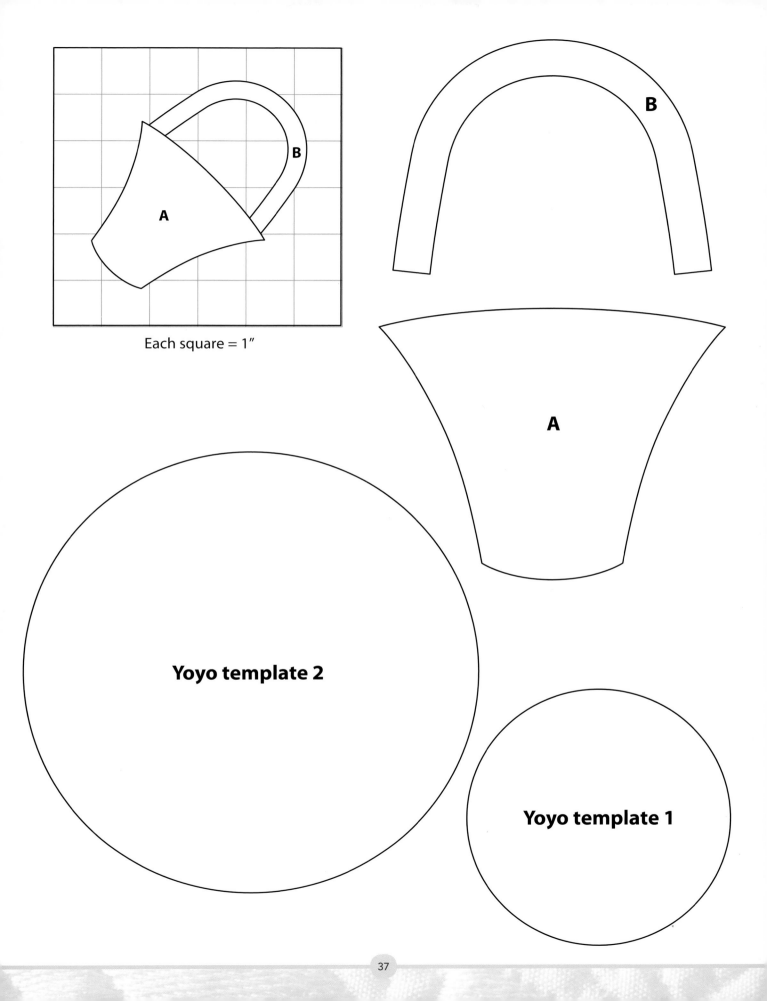

Each square = 1"

B

A

Yoyo template 2

A

B

Yoyo template 1

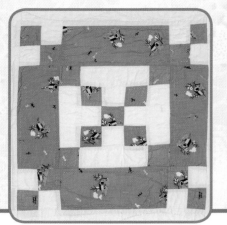

I Remember That Dress! is a perfect example of fabrics used in the 1940s. I found this quilt on eBay but could not find the pattern name. The quiltmaker and/or quilter remains unknown. Remember to add a label to your quilt!

I Remember That Dress!

(Variation of Alabama Block)
Block Size: 13½" Finished • Quilt Size: 83½" x 91½"

Fabric Needed

- 5¾ yards white or background of your choice (includes binding)
- ⅔ yard red print
- ⅔ yard blue print
- ⅔ yard black and white check
- 1 yard pink print
- ½ yard yellow print
- ⅔ yard green print

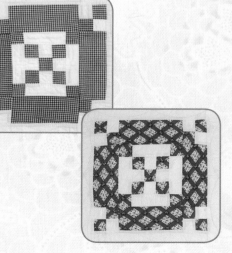

CUTTING DIRECTIONS

Note: templates are on page 43.

For EACH block, cut

- 17 – 2" squares from print fabric (template A)
- 4 – 8" x 3½" rectangles from print fabric (template B)
- 12 – 2" squares from white background fabric (template A)
- 4 – 5" x 2" rectangles from white background fabric (template C)

To Make the Block

- Using 5 print A squares and 4 white A squares, make a 9-patch center by sewing the patches together into 3 rows of 3 alternating the colors as shown below.

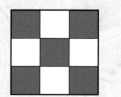

- Sew a white C rectangle to either side of the 9-patch.

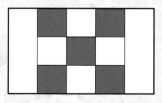

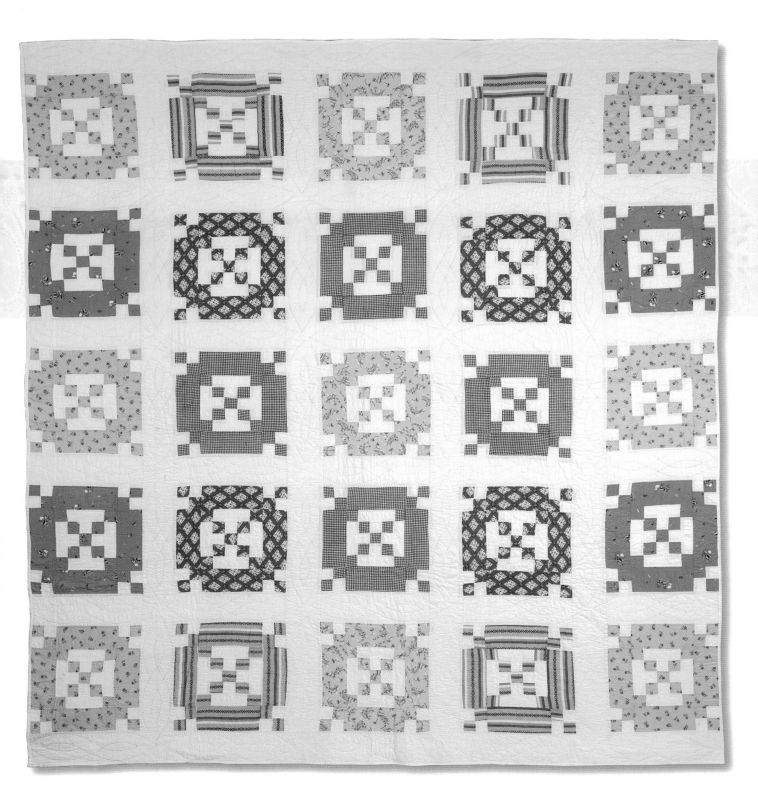

- Sew a print A square to either end of a white C rectangle. Make 2 and stitch an A/C unit to the top and the bottom of the 9-patch center.

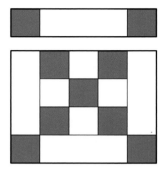

- Sew 2 print A squares and 2 white A squares together to make a 4-patch unit as shown below. Make 4.

- Sew a 4-patch unit to either end of a print B rectangle. Make 2.

- Sew a print B rectangle to either side of the 9-patch center unit.

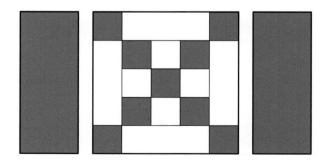

- Sew the 4-patch/C units to the top and bottom to complete the block.

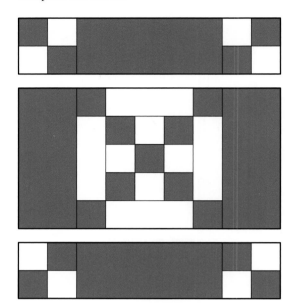

- If you use the same color layout as used in the quilt, you will need to make the following blocks:
  6 pink
  4 blue
  4 green
  4 red
  4 black and white checked
  3 yellow

PUTTING IT ALL TOGETHER

From the background fabric, cut
- 20 – 4½" x 14" rectangles for horizontal sashing strips
- 13 – 4½" strips. Stitch the strips together to make 6 – 4½" x 84" sashings – 4 will be used vertically: one will be for the top border and the other for the bottom border.
- Note: Before trimming long strips, it's a good idea to measure the sewn rows and cut to that measurement since everyone's quarter-inch seam allowance seems to vary.

- Refer to the diagram on page 42 and sew the short sashing strips and blocks into vertical rows. Each row will have 5 blocks and use 4 sashing strips. Make 5 rows.

- Sew the rows together using a long sashing strip between each row. Refer to the Assembly Diagram on page 42.

- Sew a border strip to the top and bottom of the quilt. (Again, make sure you measure through the center of the quilt before cutting the border strips. You really want this to fit correctly!)

Finishing
- Quilt and bind with background fabric.

Quilters who joined the "Mickey" Quilt Club bought kits at a reduced rated so they could earn money reselling them at the retail price. Catalogue No. 4 is shown here.

Assembly Diagram

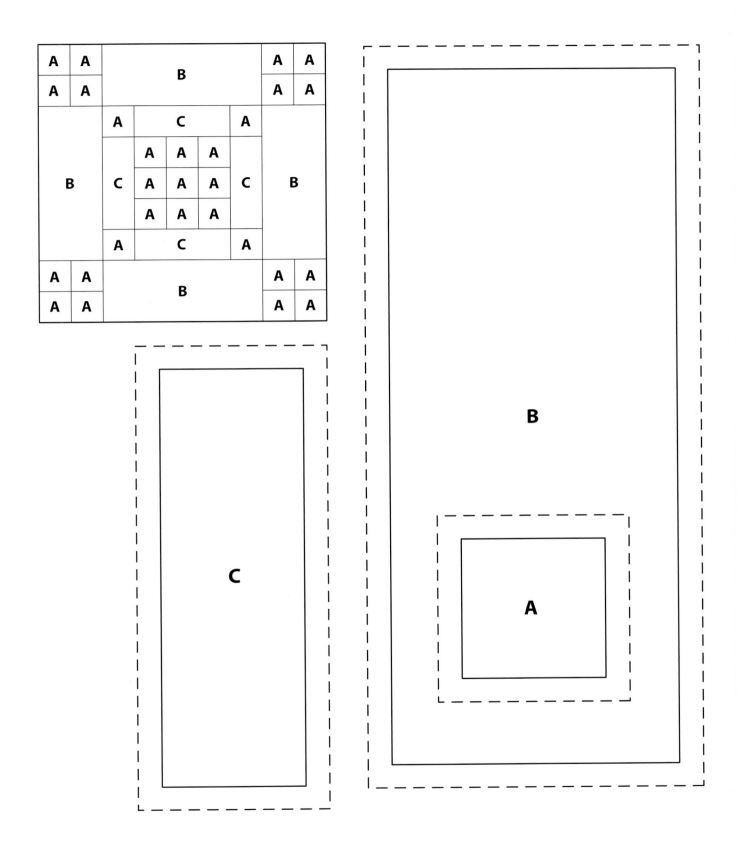

Nosegays, quiltmaker unknown, quilted by Brenda Butcher, Independence, Missouri. It's time to get out your scraps to make this beauty. "Oh, too hard," you say? Check it out, I got rid of most of those annoying set-in seams so you might just want to give this one a try.

Nosegays

Block Size: 10" Finished • Quilt Size: 82" x 96"

Fabric Needed

- 6 yards cream – background, setting blocks, side setting triangles, corner setting triangles and border
- 1¼ yards blue – nosegay cones
- 2¾ yards prints for diamonds – Use scraps but plan on having that much fabric on hand when cutting the diamonds – this includes the diamonds used for the outer border.
- ¾ yard prints for triangles in bouquet – Use scraps as above
- 1 yard blue print for binding

CUTTING INSTRUCTIONS

Note: templates are on pages 49-50.

From the cream colored fabric, cut

- 90 rectangles using template A – You'll need 3 for each block
- 90 rectangles using template B – 3 per block
- 120 triangles using template C – 4 per block
- 60 triangles using template D – 2 per block
- 30 triangles using template E – 1 per block
- 30 triangles using template F – 1 per block
- 20 – 10½" squares for setting blocks
- 5 – 15½" squares – Cut each square from corner to corner twice on the diagonal for side setting triangles. (You will have 2 triangles left over. Save them for another project.)
- 2 – 8" squares – Cut each square from corner to corner once on the diagonal for corner setting triangles.
- 9 – 4" strips across the width of the fabric for outer borders

From blue fabric, cut

- 30 triangles using template G – 1 per block
- 30 triangles using template K – 1 per block

From the print scraps, cut

- 180 diamonds using template H – 6 per block
- 114 diamonds using template H – outside pieced borders
- 90 squares using template J – 3 per block
- 120 triangles using template C – 4 per block

Nosegays Continued

To Make the Block

The following directions are for making one block. You will need to make 30 blocks.

- Sew a cream C triangle to a print C triangle.

- Sew a print J square to a cream B rectangle. Add a cream A rectangle as shown.

- Sew a cream D triangle to an H diamond.

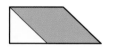

- Sew an A/B/J unit to an H/D unit as shown below.

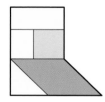

- Sew a C/C unit to an H diamond.

- Sew the 2 pieces together being careful not to sew into the seam allowance. Raise the presser foot of your sewing machine and align the seam allowance with the edge of the diamond.

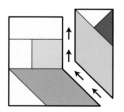

- Make the upper left corner of the block. Sew a C/C unit to an H diamond.

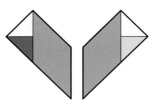

- Sew a corner A/B/J unit to an H/C/C unit. Add the H/C/C diamond as above, being careful not to sew into the seam allowance.

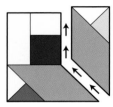

- Make the upper right corner of the block. Sew a C/C unit to an H diamond. Add an A/B/J unit. Set aside for the moment. Sew a D triangle to an H diamond. Now sew the 2 units together as shown below.

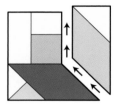

- Sew a blue K triangle to an F cream triangle. Sew a cream E triangle to a blue G triangle. Sew the 2 units together.

- Sew the 4 units together to make the block. Make 30 blocks.

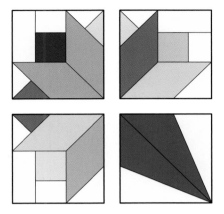

Quilt Assembly

- Refer to the Assembly Diagram on page 48 and sew the rows together on the diagonal adding in the setting triangles and setting blocks where needed.

Borders

- Measure the quilt top through the center horizontally. To that measurement, add 14". (We are using our 4" cream colored strips we cut across the width of the fabric for our borders and have added twice the width of the strip – 8" + 6" to accommodate the miter.) Make 2 strips this size. Begin pinning at the center of the quilt and pin to the seam allowance on each edge. Stitch in place being careful not to run past the seam allowance (start and stop ¼" from edge).

- Measure the quilt top through the center vertically. Follow the same instructions as above to make the correct size borders. Stitch in place leaving the overlapping edges free.

- Again, measure the top horizontally through the center. Sew the diamond border together. You should need 26 diamonds for each top and bottom border. If this border doesn't quite fit, take a few of the seam lines in. It really won't be noticeable. Sew one diamond border to the top cream border of the quilt, the other to the bottom cream border.

- Again, measure the top vertically through the center. Sew the diamond border together. You should need 31 diamonds for each side border. If this border doesn't quite fit, take a few of the seam lines in. It really won't be noticeable. Sew a diamond border to each cream border on the sides of the quilt.

- Mark the miter on the reverse side of each border using a 45-degree angle. Match the marks up and sew from the inside of each corner to the outer edge. Trim the seam allowance to ¼".

Finishing

- Quilt and bind.

Assembly Diagram

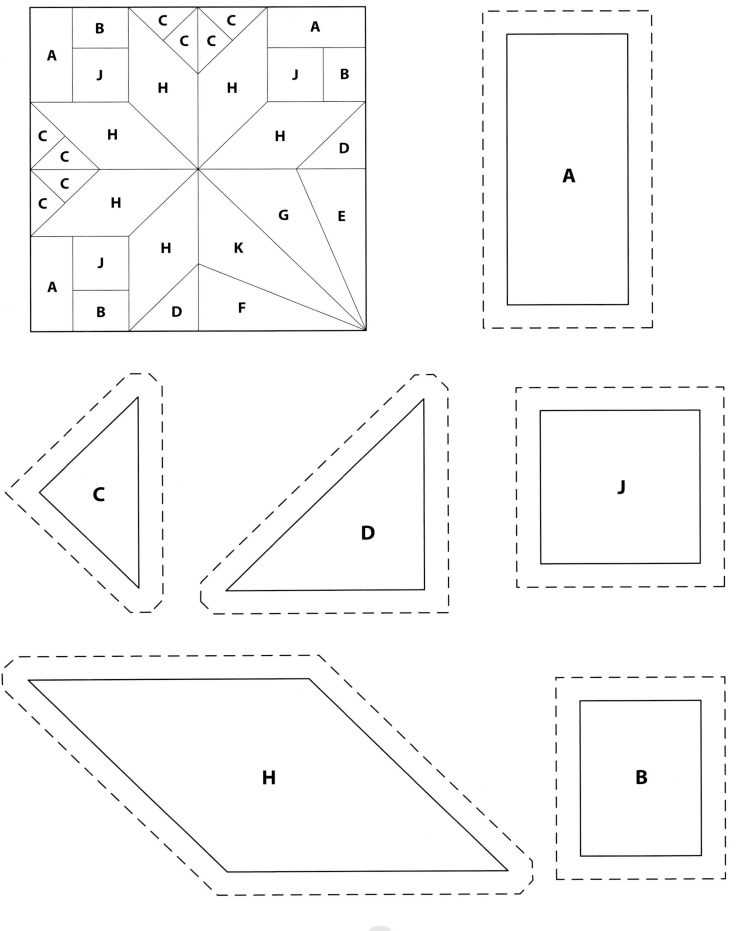

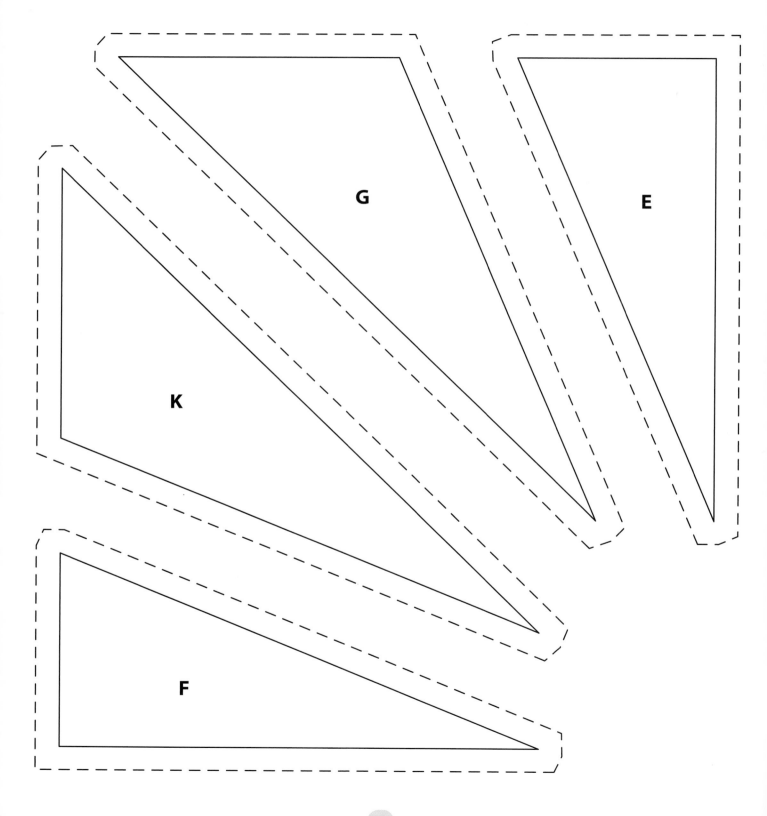

G

E

K

F

inspection...

then the stamp of quality

As each garment comes off the line it is thoroughly inspected for construction and fit by critical and experienced tailors. Only when it has passed this final, vigorous examination may it carry the Betty Rose label.

Even here, in our huge shipping room, every order is filled with characteristic care.

Betty Rose ad touting the inspection process each garment went through before leaving the factory.

Betty Rose

behind the label...
...the inside story*

1 Extra-wide lap-over prevents gapping.

2 Specially molded shoulder pads carefully placed for a softer contour.

3 Fronts felled to prevent rolling.

4 Extra turnover at waist bands and at coat and skirt bottoms to allow ample lengthening.

5 All points of strain reinforced with tape for strength and long wear.

6 Sleeve lining secured in place by accurate felling, plus extra turnover for lengthening.

7 Open bottoms insure perfect drape.

8 Full-cut linings are back-pleated for fullness and to hold shape.

9 Collars and lapels are canvas interlined for better fit.

10 Accurately placed floating tacks guarantee natural drape.

The Betty Rose label is your hallmark of quality, representing fine quality fabrics and quality construction throughout. This is the famous "Inside Story" — ten features of superior construction — built into only a Betty Rose coat or suit!

*The "Inside Story" is a registered trade-mark of the Sterns-Slegman-Prins Company.

Klonda Holt of Overland Park, Kansas, made this version of Starry Path using hand-dyed fabrics from Cherrywood Fabrics, Inc. It was quilted by Brenda Butcher of Independence, Missouri.

Starry Path

Block Size: 10" Finished • Quilt Size: 49"

Fabric Needed

- ½ yard each of 8 different colors
- 3 yards black for background
- ¾ yard black for binding

INSTRUCTIONS

- This quilt is paper pieced and uses 16 – 10" blocks and 4 – 4½" blocks in the border. Eight of the 10" blocks are made alike using the same 4 colors in the star. The other 8 – 10" blocks are made alike using the remaining 4 colors of fabric. For the sake of clarity we will call them Block A and Block B.

- Two of the 4½" corner blocks match Block A and the other 2 match Block B.

- Make 16 copies of the pattern on pages 57 and 59. Each block has 4 sections; A, B, C and D.

- Make 4 copies of the 4½" blocks on page 58.

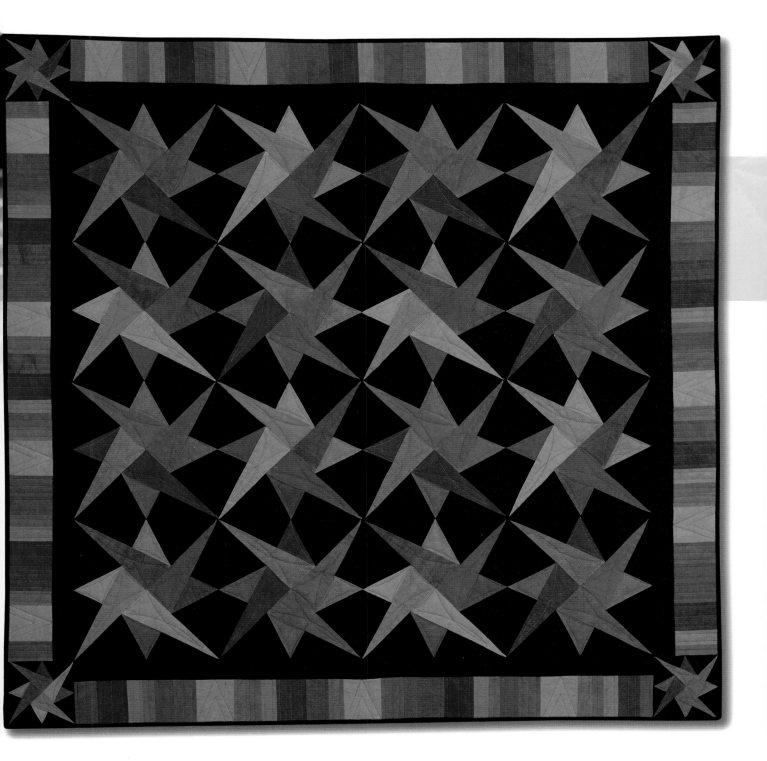

Block A

Section A
- Position A1 – Black – 5½" x 4½"
- Position A2 – Blue/Green – 4½" x 3"
- Position A3 – Black – 3½" x 5½"
- Position A4 – Rust – 8½" x 3"

Section B
- Position B1 – Black – 5½" x 4½"
- Position B2 – Light Blue – 4½" x 3"
- Position B3 – Black – 3½" x 5½"
- Position B4 – Gold – 8½" x 3"

Section C
- Position C1 – Black – 5½" x 4½"
- Position C2 – Rust – 4½" x 3"
- Position C3 – Black – 3½" x 5½"
- Position C4 – Light Blue – 8½" x 3"

Section D
- Position D1 – Black – 5½" x 4½"
- Position D2 – Gold – 4½" x 3"
- Position D3 – Black – 3½" x 5½"
- Position D4 – Blue/Green – 8½" x 3"

Block B

Section A
- Position A1 – Black – 5½" x 4½"
- Position A2 – Olive Green – 4½" x 3"
- Position A3 – Black – 3½" x 5½"
- Position A4 – Wine – 8½" x 3"

Section B
- Position B1 – Black – 5½" x 4½"
- Position B2 – Dark Gold – 4½" x 3"
- Position B3 – Black – 3½" x 5½"
- Position B4 – Dark Blue – 8½" x 3"

Section C
- Position C1 – Black – 5½" x 4½"
- Position C2 – Wine – 4½" x 3"
- Position C3 – Black – 3½" x 5 ½"
- Position C4 – Dark Gold – 8½" x 3"

Section D
- Position D1 – Black – 5 ½" x 4 ½"
- Position D2 – Dark Blue – 4½" x 3"
- Position D3 – Black – 3½" x 5½"
- Position D4 – Olive Green – 8½" x 3"

Follow the same color positions for the small blocks and make 2 of each.
- Position 1 in each section needs to be cut 3" x 2½"
- Position 2 in each section needs to be cut 3" x 2"
- Position 3 in each section needs to be cut 3" x 2"
- Position 4 in each section needs to be cut 4" x 2"

- Sew section D to A.

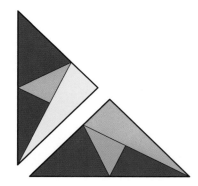

- Sew section B to C.

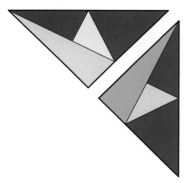

- Sew the DA section to the BC section.

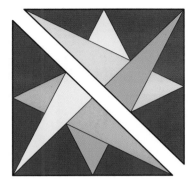

Quilt Assembly

- Refer to the quilt photo on page 53 and sew the blocks together, alternating Block A and B. Notice that they are turned in different directions.

Borders

- Measure the quilt top through the center. Cut 2" strips across the width of the black fabric by that measurement. Make 4.

- Cut random width strips across the eight fabrics you have chosen for your blocks. Sew the strips together. Cut the strips into 3½" increments. Sew enough 3½" units together to equal the width of the quilt top to make the piano key border. Make 4.

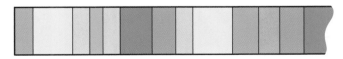

- Sew a black 2" strip to one side of the piano keys.

- Sew a border to each side of the quilt.

- Sew a small Starry Path block to each end of the 2 remaining border strips.

- Sew one strip to the top and one to the bottom of the quilt.

Finishing

- Layer the quilt with backing and batting and quilt. Bind to complete the quilt.

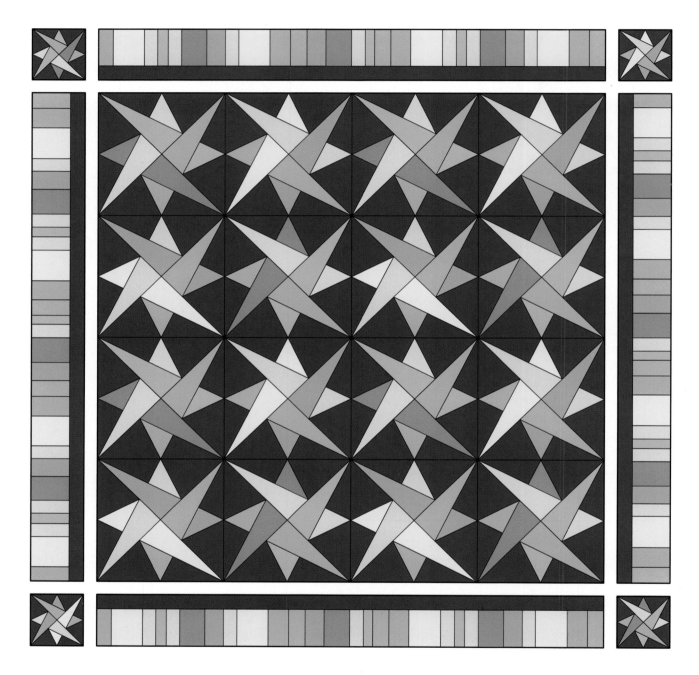

Assembly Diagram

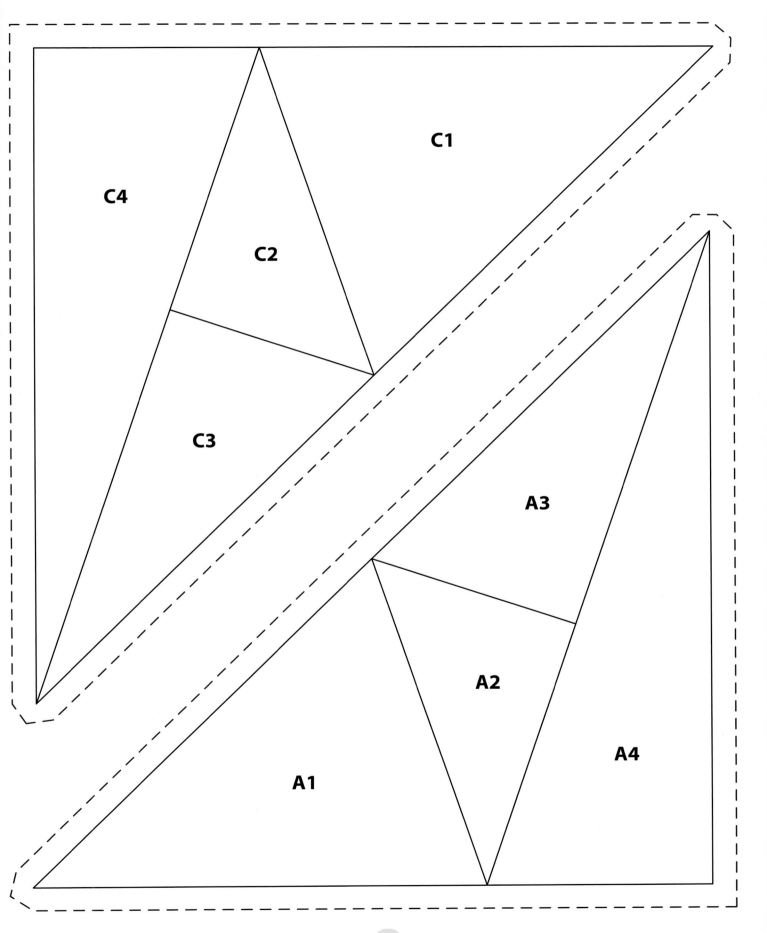

C1

C4

C2

C3

A3

A2

A1

A4

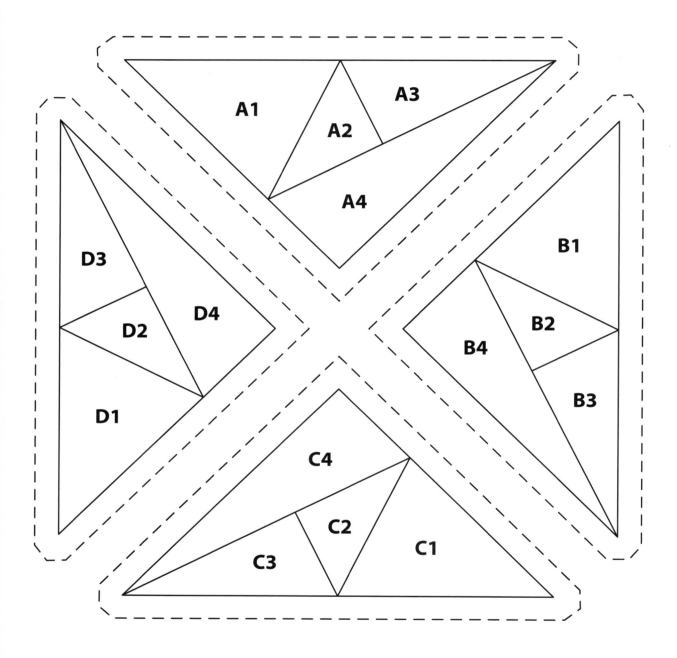

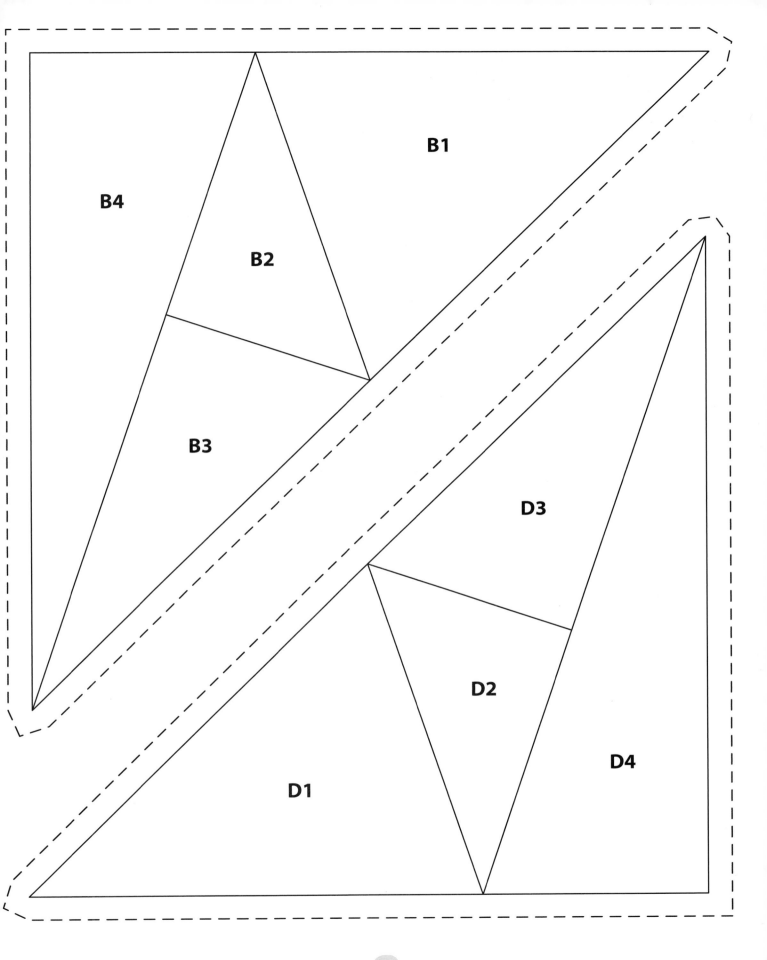

Even though Mother's Choice is the traditional name for this quilt, I'm calling it Petticoat Lane after one of the streets in the Garment District in Kansas City. I purchased it on eBay. Our unknown quilter made excellent use of her turquoise scraps, a fashionable color during the '40s. I love the graphic look of this quilt but wanted to do away with all those inset seams. By dividing the block into four quadrants, this quilt becomes a snap to piece!

Petticoat Lane

Block Size: 9" Finished • Quilt Size: 73" x 86.5"

Fabric Needed

- 4¼ yards of cream for background
- 1 fat quarter yellow/black plaid
- 1 fat quarter of one purple print
- ⅓ yard of another purple print
- ½ yard one turquoise
- ¾ yard of another turquoise
- ½ yard black on white print
- 1¼ yards purple floral print
- ⅔ yard green plaid
- ⅔ yard brown floral
- ½ yard blue paisley
- ½ yard white on black print
- 1 yard red plaid
- 1 yard cream for bias binding

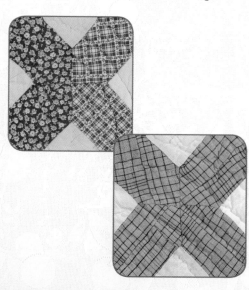

CUTTING INSTRUCTIONS

From the cream background fabric, cut

- 47 – 3" strips across the width of the fabric.
  Cut the strips into 3" squares. You need 608 squares and each strip yields 13.

- From each of the prints, you will need to cut 4 - 5" squares per block. There are half-blocks at the bottom of the quilt. For each half-block, you will need to cut 2 – 5" squares.

- 1 full block and 1 half-block are made using yellow/black plaid
- 2 blocks use one purple print
- 4 blocks use the other purple print
- 5 blocks are made from one turquoise
- 8 full blocks and 2 half-blocks are made from the second turquoise
- 6 blocks are made using the black on white print
- 12 full blocks and 1 half-block are made using the purple floral print
- 11 full blocks and 1 half-block are made using the red plaid
- 7 full blocks are made using the green plaid
- 6 full blocks and 1 half-block use the brown floral fabric.
- 5 full blocks and 1 half-block use the blue paisley fabric.
- 5 full blocks and 1 half-block are made using the white on black print.

To Make the Block

- Fold 2 cream squares in half on the diagonal and finger press the crease in place. Pin each to opposing corners of a print square with right sides facing.

- Sew along the crease then trim ¼" away from the seam.

- Press the block with the seam allowance going toward the dark fabric.

- Make 4 units per full block and 2 per half-block.

- Sew the 4 units together to complete the block.

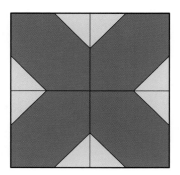

Quilt Assembly

- When the blocks are complete, refer to the Assembly Diagram on the next page and sew the rows together.

Finishing

- Layer the top with backing and batting and quilt. Bind with bias binding.

Assembly Diagram

Flower Pot, quiltmaker and quilter, unknown. This 1940s quilt was pieced and quilted by hand. The fabric used in this quilt is a study in what was in fashion during that era. Feel free to trade out the orange used for the basket or pot for colors of your choosing.

Flower Pot

Block Size: 10" Finished • Quilt Size: 85" x 85"

Fabric Needed
- 7 yards cream (Includes binding)
- 1¼ yard orange
- 2¼ yards assorted prints

CUTTING INSTRUCTIONS
Note: templates are on page 69.

From the cream colored fabric, cut
- 72 – 6½" x 2½" rectangles or use template C
- 126 – 2⅞" squares – Cut each square from corner to corner once on the diagonal or use template A.
- 18 – 4⅞" squares – Cut each square from corner to corner once on the diagonal or use template B.
- 25 – 10½" squares – These will be used for setting blocks.
- 5 – 15½" squares – Cut each square from corner to corner twice on the diagonal. These are your side setting triangles.
- 2 – 8" squares – Cut each square from corner to corner once on the diagonal and set aside. These are your corner setting triangles.

From the assorted prints, cut
- 288 – 2⅞" squares – Cut each square from corner to corner once on the diagonal or use template A.

From the orange fabric, cut
- 36 – 2⅞" squares – Cut each square from corner to corner once on the diagonal or use template A.
- 18 – 6⅞" squares – Cut each square from corner to corner once on the diagonal or use template D.

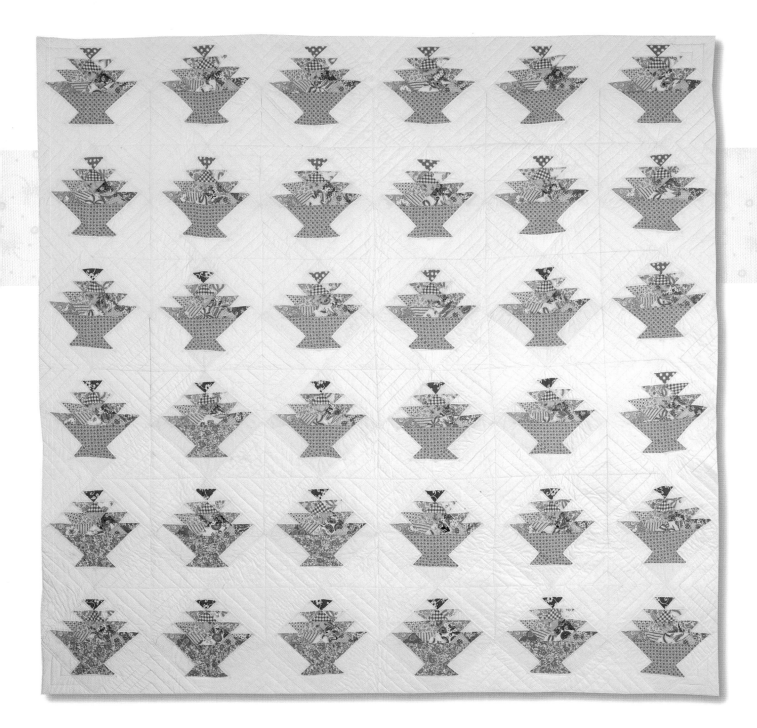

To Make Each Block

- Pair a cream A triangle with a print A triangle and sew along the diagonal edge to make a half-square triangle. Make 7.

- Pair 2 print A triangles and sew together to make a half-square triangle. Make 3.

- Sew an orange A triangle to a cream C rectangle. Make 2 and they must be a mirror image of each other as shown below.

- Sew 4 cream/print half-square triangles together as shown.

- Sew a cream/print half-square triangle to 2 print half-square triangles. Add a print triangle to complete the row.

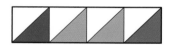

- The next row is made by sewing a cream/print half-square triangle to a print half-square triangle unit. Add a print triangle to finish the row.

- The final row of "flowers" is made by sewing a cream/print half-square triangle unit to a print triangle.

- Sew the rows together as shown.

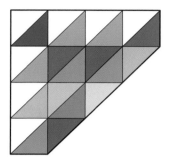

- Add the orange D triangle.

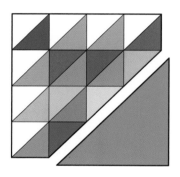

- Stitch the C/A units in place.

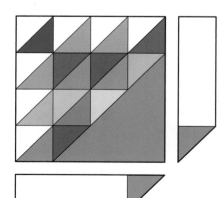

- Add the cream B triangle to complete the block.

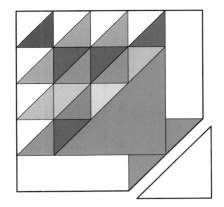

- Make 36 blocks.

Quilt Assembly
- Follow the Assembly Diagram on the next page and sew the rows together on the diagonal. Add in the setting triangles and corner triangles where necessary.

Finishing
- Layer the quilt top with batting and backing and quilt.

According to the 1953 Kansas City city directory, this building on the corner of 10th and Broadway was home to Ti-Pi Company, Rose Mercantile Company, Lan Mar Manufacturing Company, Jenny Garments, Inc, Herdan Morris, Inc, Danny Dare Boys Wear, Inc and Vic-Gene Manufacturing Company. Each business occupied one floor of the building.

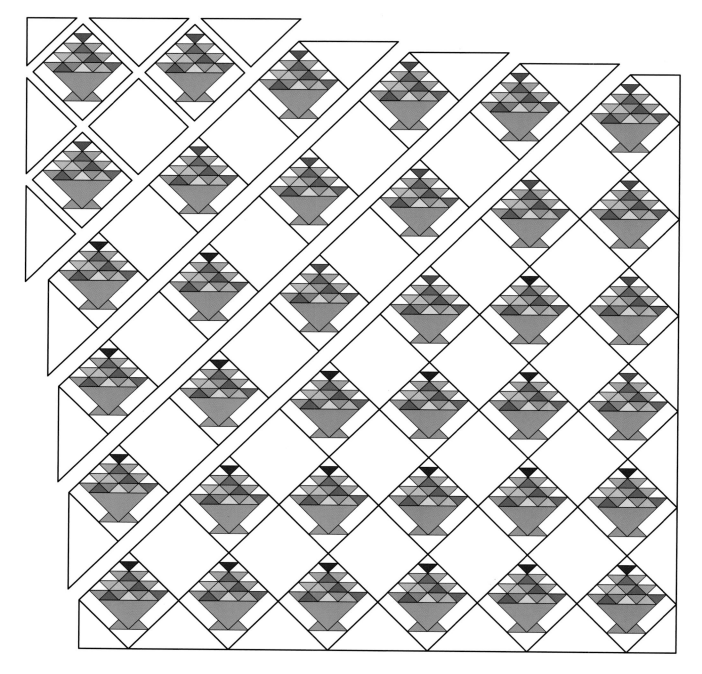

Assembly Diagram

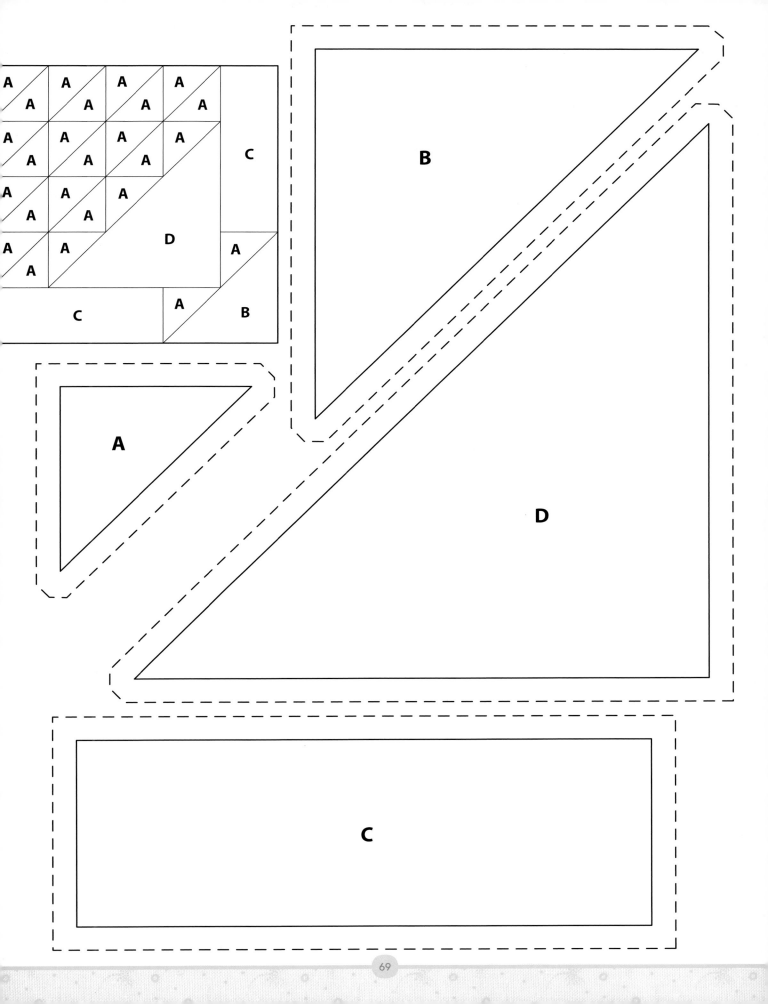

Fan Quilt hand stitched and hand quilted by Edie McGinnis. Much of the fabric used in the fans are scraps from the Princess Peggy dress factory in Peoria, Illinois.

Fan Quilt

Block Size: 9" Finished • Quilt Size: 83½" x 95"

Fabric Needed

- 6¼ yards dark green – includes 1 yard for binding
- 2¼ yards light green
- Enough scraps to equal 2¼ yards

CUTTING INSTRUCTIONS

Note: template is on page 72.

From the dark green fabric, cut
- 42 – 9½" squares
- 56 – 3" squares for sashing cornerstones
- Set aside the remainder of the green for your borders and binding

From the light green fabric, cut
- 97 – 3" x 9½" strips

From the scraps, cut
- 210 fan blades using template A

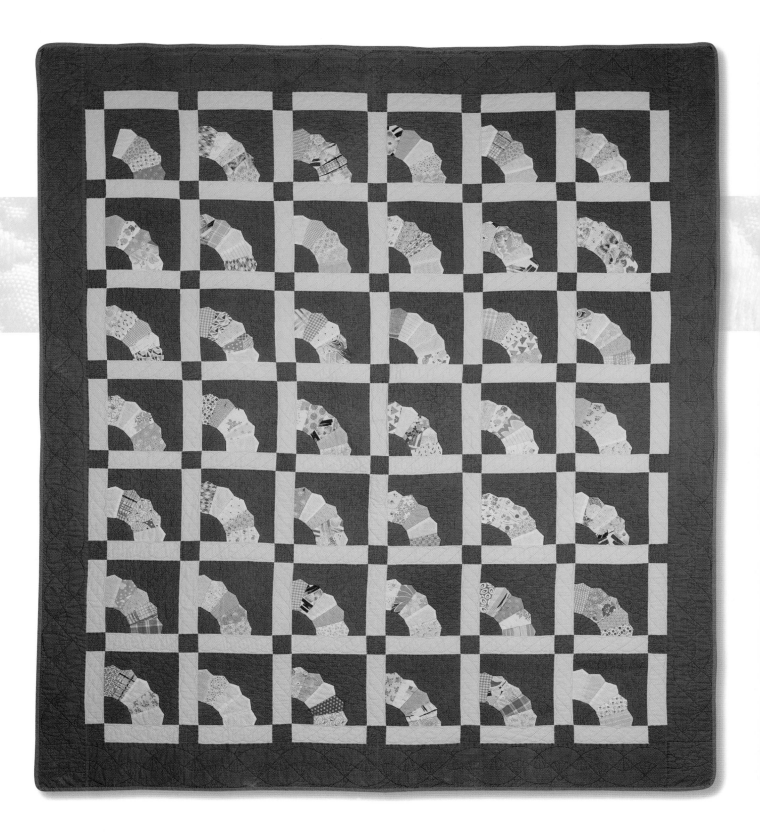

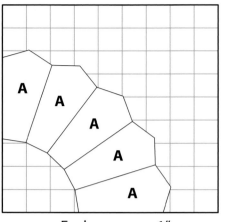

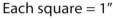

Each square = 1"

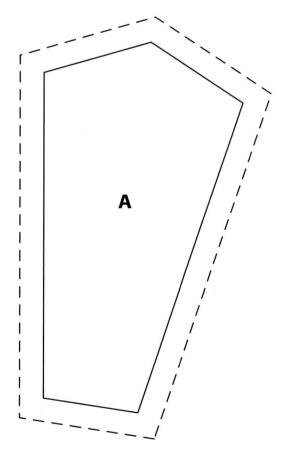

To Make Each Block

- Sew 5 fan blades together. Turn the edges under on the top and along the curve and pin in place. Appliqué the fans in place using your favorite method. Make 42 blocks.

- Sew a row of cornerstones and sashing strips together. You need to begin and end with a cornerstone. The row should have 7 cornerstones and 6 sashing strips. Make 8 rows like this.

- Sew a sashing strip to a fan block. Add another sashing strip. Continue on in this manner until you have a row of 6 blocks and 7 sashing strips. Make 7 rows.

- Sew the cornerstone/sashing strip rows to the rows of blocks. Refer to the Assembly Diagram on the next page if necessary.

Borders

- Measure the top through the center from top to bottom. Make 2 border strips this length by 6½" wide. Sew one border to each side.

- Now measure the top through the center from side to side. Make 2 border strips this length by 6½" wide. Sew one to the top and one to the bottom of the quilt.

Finishing

- Layer the quilt top with batting and backing. Quilt and bind.

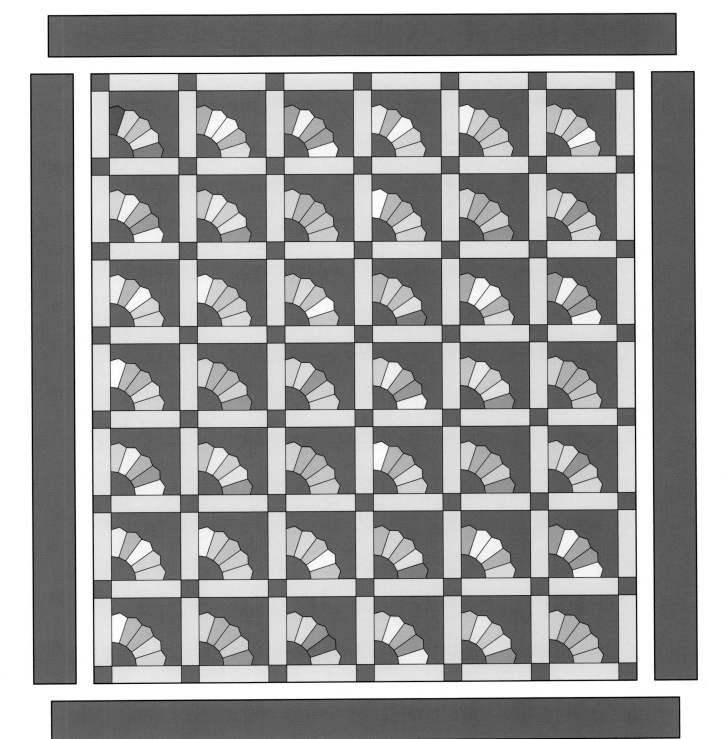

Assembly Diagram

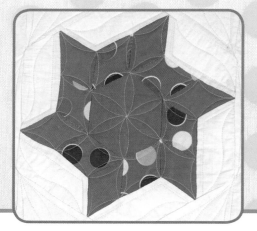

I bought this quilt top on eBay. Only when it was hanging on the wall as we were doing the photo shoot for this book, did I notice it seemed to be missing a long row of blocks. You will notice the large polka-dot fabric is repeated in three different color ways. Scraps from a factory, perhaps?

Pinwheels

Block Size: 10" Finished • Quilt Size: 90" x 90"
This includes a long row we've added (see page 80) to make the quilt symmetrical.

Fabric Needed
- 5¼ yards background fabric
- Enough solid scraps for the hexagons and diamonds to equal 3 yards of fabric
- Enough print scraps to equal 2⅓ yards of fabric
- 1 yard blue for bias binding

CUTTING INSTRUCTIONS
Note: templates are on page 79-80.

From the background fabric, cut
- 152 triangles using the triangle template on page 80 – You will be able to get 13 triangles per strip if you flip the template from top to bottom as you cut.
- 462 pieces using template C

From the solid scraps, cut
- 77 hexagons using template B
- 462 diamonds using template A

From the print scraps, cut
- 462 diamonds using template A

To Make Each Block

- Sew a print A diamond to a solid A diamond. Make 6.

- We are going to use a method called "partial seaming" as we sew this block together. And, quite frankly, I would make this quilt my hand-piecing project until it came to sewing the rows together.

- Sew a diamond unit to the center hexagon with the solid diamond touching the hexagon. Do not sew the seam all the way, rather begin in the center leaving the bottom portion unsewn.

Leave bottom
of seam open

- Add the next set of diamonds, sewing in a counterclockwise direction.

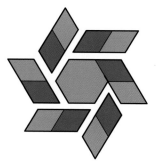

- Continue on around the center hexagon until all the diamond units are sewn in place. Now go back and stitch the seam you left open closed.

- Inset the background C pieces into the block. Make 77 blocks.

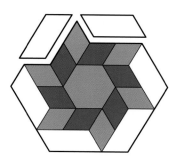

Quilt Assembly

- After all your blocks have been completed, you will need to sew them into rows. Sew 2 background triangles to the first block. Add another block. Sew 2 more triangles in place. Add another block. Continue on this way until you have sewn 9 blocks together. This makes a long row and you will need 5 rows made like this.

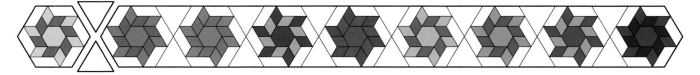

- To make the alternating shorter rows, begin by sewing 2 triangles to the block.

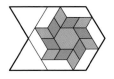

- Add 2 triangles to the opposite side of the block.

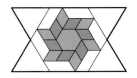

- Add another block and continue on in this manner until you have sewn 8 blocks together. End the row with 2 background triangles. Make 4 rows like this.

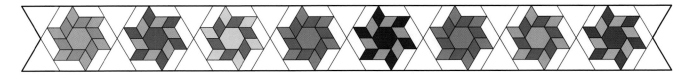

Finishing

- Refer to the Assembly Diagram on the next page and sew the rows together. Layer the top with batting and backing. Quilt and bind.

Assembly Diagram

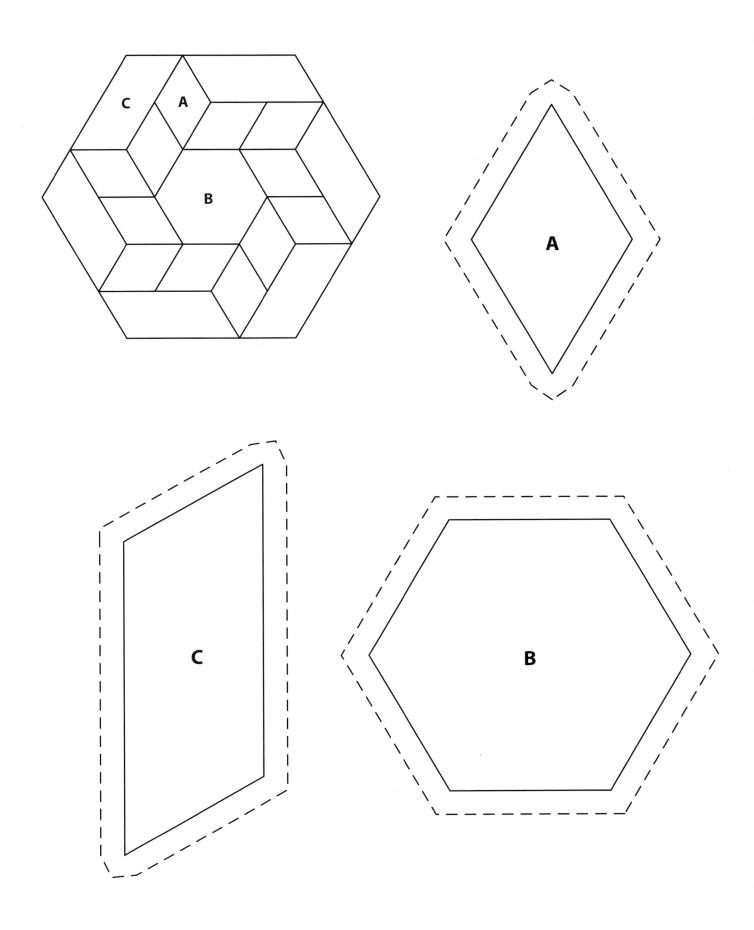

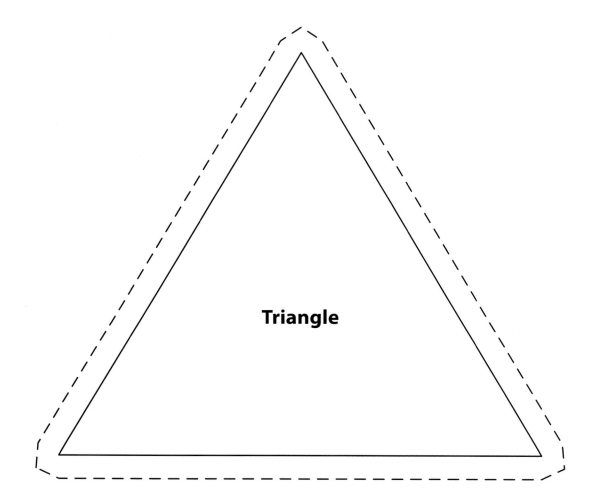

Triangle

A sampling of ads featuring popular companies located in Kansas City's Garment District.

Projects

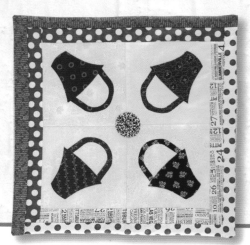

Supplies

- 16" pillow form
- 1 – 6½" strip of background fabric
- 1 – 7½" strip of red fabric for baskets – or use scraps
- 1 – 1½" strip of 2 different red on cream prints
- 1 – 1½" strip of 2 different cream on red prints
- 1 – 6½" square of cream on red print for yoyo
- 1 – 10½" strip of red on cream fabric for the back of the pillow

Basket Throw Pillow

Made by Edie McGinnis • Pillow Size: 16" Square

INSTRUCTIONS

- Refer to the instructions on page 32 for making basket blocks. Make 4.

- Sew the 4 blocks together. Refer to the photo if necessary.

- Cut 1 – 1½" x 12½" strip of red on cream fabric and sew to the basket block.

- Cut 1 – 1½" x 13½" strip of red on cream fabric and sew it to one side of the pillow. It should butt up against the previous strip.

- Cut 1 – 1½" x 13½" strip of cream on red print. Sew it to the other side of the pillow.

- Cut 1 – 1½" x 14½" strip of cream on red print. Sew it to the remaining side of the pillow.

- Cut 1 – 1½" x 14½" strip of red on cream fabric and sew to the bottom of the block.

- Cut 1 – 1½" x 15½" strip of red on cream fabric and sew it to one side of the pillow. It should butt up against the previous strip.

- Cut 1 – 1½" x 15½" strip of cream on red print. Sew it to the other side of the pillow.

- Cut 1 – 1½" x 16½" strip of cream on red print. Sew it to the remaining side of the pillow.

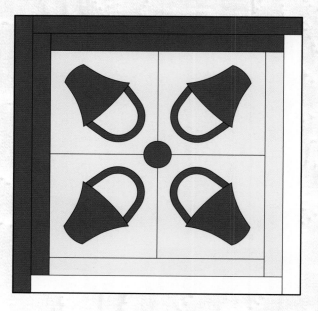

- Make 1 large cream on red yoyo. You'll find the template on page 37.

- Sew the yoyo to the center intersection of the pillow. (That's where the 4 seams of the basket blocks meet.)

- Cut 2 – 16½" x 10½" rectangles from the backing fabric. Press under a ¼" seam allowance on each rectangle. Then press under a 1½" seam allowance and stitch across the piece.

- Pin the 2 pieces to the reverse side of the pillow top. The 2 will overlap. Stitch all around the pillow, then turn it right side out.

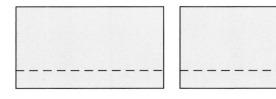

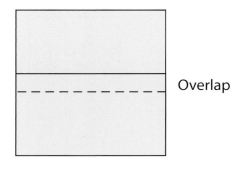

Overlap

- Stuff with the pillow form.

I bought a decorative hook from Hobby Lobby but you can make this cute little project from scratch if you can't find a ready-made one.

Robe Hook

Supplies

- 1 – 5" x ¼" square of wood
- 1 hook
- 1 cork knob if desired
- Paint – should match basket fabric
- Varnish
- Foam brush
- 6½" square of fabric for background
- 8" square of red on cream fabric for basket
- 4" square of red on cream fabric for yoyo.
- 2 – 5" squares of batting
- 5" square of lightweight cardboard
- Hot glue gun and glue sticks
- Picture hanger

INSTRUCTIONS

- Refer to the directions on page 32 and make 1 basket block and 1 small yoyo. Applique the yoyo to the basket.

- Paint the square of wood and the knob with 2 coats of paint. Let dry between coats then varnish.

- Mount the hook and the picture hanger on the back of the block of wood. You may have to gouge out some of the back so the hook will nestle into the back and not make the project wobble.

- Place the batting squares and the basket block over the cardboard square. Turn the raw edges to the back and glue to the cardboard. Let dry.

- Glue the cardboard-backed basket block to the wood and let dry. Hang on the wall.

Night Light

Here's a quick project just in case you got carried away while making yoyos.

Supplies
- Small lamp with shade
- Fabric for yoyos – the amount of yoyos needed is contingent upon the measurement of the base of the lampshade
- Hot glue gun and glue sticks

INSTRUCTIONS
- Measure the base of the shade. Divide that number by 4 and mark each measurement on the lampshade.

- Using the hot glue gun, glue a yoyo at each mark.

- Fill in the rest of the way around the shade by gluing yoyos all the way around the bottom of the shade.

- If you like, you can add yoyos to the top of the shade as well.

My friend Brenda Butcher came up with the idea and design for this sweet little trinket box. You'll find Brenda's name all over this book. She's the talented quilter who makes my quilts look so beautiful.

Yoyo Trinket Box

Supplies

- Round paper mache box – The box we used 2¼" in diameter and 1¾" tall but these instructions will work for any size you chose to use.
- Fabric scraps
- Ribbon or trim
- Lightweight cardboard or template plastic
- Acrylic paint to match fabric
- Water-based varnish
- Small foam brush
- Glue stick

INSTRUCTIONS

- Paint the inside and the lid of the box with 2 coats of acrylic paint. Set aside and let dry. Apply one coat of water-based varnish and set aside to dry.

- Trace the bottom and the lid of the box onto lightweight cardboard or template plastic.

To Make the Yoyo on the Lid

- Glue about 1" square of fabric to the center of the cardboard circle you traced from the lid.

- Double the measurement across the lid and add ½". Fold the fabric under ¼" and run a basting stitch around the edge. Place the cardboard circle that has the glued patch of fabric inside and pull the thread tight to form a yoyo. Knot off the thread. Glue to the top of lid. Note: you will not be removing the cardboard circle.

Covering the Box Base

- Measure around the outside of the box. Multiply that number by 2 to determine the length of fabric you will need to go around the box. Measure the box from top to bottom and add ¾". Sew the short sides together to create a tube. Baste around both raw edges. Draw up to fit around the box and knot off your threads. Bring the top of the tube over the top of box to the inside and glue in place. Glue a piece of ribbon or trim over the raw edge. Glue the other raw edge to the bottom of the box.

Fabric Circle for Bottom of Box

- Measure across the bottom of the box and add ½". Baste around the edge. Place the bottom cardboard circle inside and draw up the fabric to fit and knot off your thread. Glue to the bottom of the box covering all raw edges.

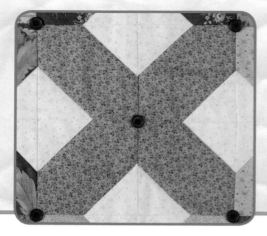

Table topper made and quilted by Edie McGinnis. You can update the look of the Petticoat Lane quilt by using one of today's fabric lines. This project was made using Blueberry Crumb Cake fabric designed by Blackbird Designs for Moda.

Petticoat Lane Table Topper

Block Size: 9" Finished • Table Topper Size: 27" Square

Supplies

- 10" square of each color of fabric. Cut each square into fourths (You should end up with 4 - 5" squares.)
- 21" background fabric
- ⅓ yard dark blue for binding
- 13 brown buttons

INSTRUCTIONS

- Refer to the directions for making the blocks on page 62. Make 9 blocks. I made three blocks shaded brown, 2 dark blue/brown print, 2 medium blue/brown print and 2 light blue.

- Refer to the photo and sew the blocks into 3 rows of three. Sew the rows together.

- Layer with backing and batting and quilt. Bind to complete the quilt.

- Sew a dark brown button in the center of each square and at each junction where the blocks meet.

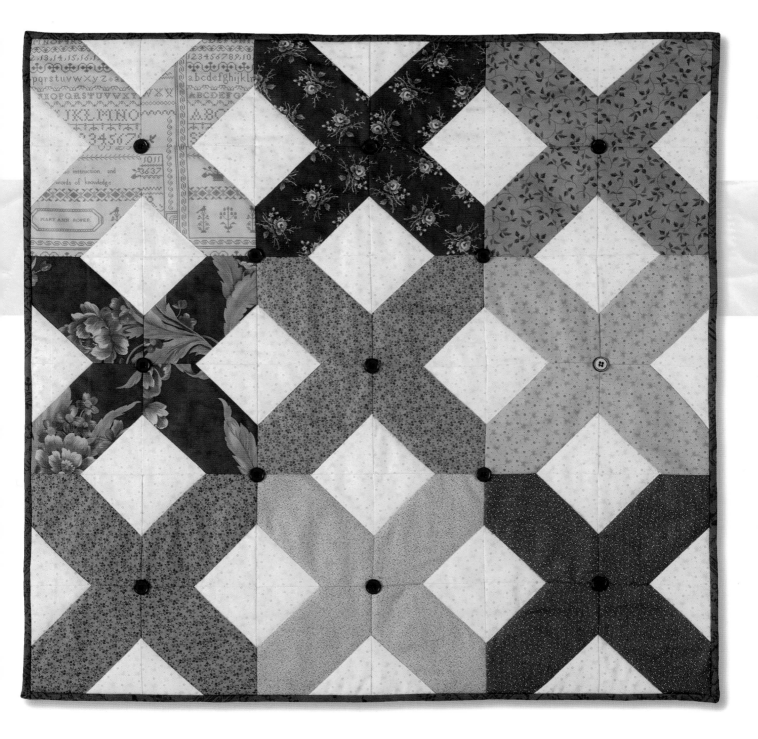

Resources

Books and Magazines

American Quilts in the Modern Age 1870-1940. Nebraska: University of Nebraska Press, 2009.

Carleton, Jetta, and R.D. Palmer. *Fashion for the Middle Millions.* Kansas City: Swing, 1947.

Cressionnie, Elaine. *The Princess Peggy Dress Factory.* Quilt Magazine, Winter, 1990.

DeAngelo, Dory. *Employee Strikes Weave an Historic Thread Through Kansas City.* Northeast News, 2008.

Donohue, James. *Greater Kansas City Official Year Book, 1904-05.* Kansas City: 1905.

Ford, Margot. *Called to Courage.* Columbia: University of Missouri Press, 2002.

Jackson, James. *Little Known Industries of Greater Kansas City, 1926-1929.* Kansas City: 1929.

Kansas City Centennial Association. *Fashions Go Out of Date Too — But in Kansas City They Are Up to the Minute.* Kansas City: Kansas City Centennial Souvenir Program, 1950.

Merwin, Pearl. *American System of Dressmaking.* Kansas City: The American College of Dressmaking, 1907.

O'Dwyer, Tom. *Hot Cargo.* True Detective Magazine, Volume 40, No. 5, Aug. 1943.

Show Me Missouri Women. Kirksville: Thomas Jefferson University Press, 1989.

The Garment Industry of Greater Kansas City: Report No. 5. Kansas City: Research and Information Department Report, 1945.

Waldvogel, Merikay, and Barbara Brackman. *Patchwork Souvenirs of the 1933 World's Fair.* Nashville: Rutledge Hill Press, 1993.

Newspapers

The Kansas City Star, May 07, 2006. p. 30. Star Magazine. Burnes, Brian. "The Nelly Don Affair."

The Kansas City Star, September 29, 2002. p. 12. Engle, Tim. "The Faded Garment District."

The Kansas City Star, November 8, 2009. p. 14. Star Magazine. Cole, Suzanne. "Museum Honors KC's Fashionable Past."

The Kansas City Star, February 21, 2011. p. F10. Barnhart, Aaron. "A Timely Look at Labor's Birth; As Unions Make Headlines, PBS' 'American Experience' Examines the Triangle Shirtwaist Factory Fire."

The Kansas City Star, April 29, 1896. "Story of a Merchant."

The Kansas City Star, January 1, 2000. p. E2. Montgomery, Rick. "On the Job."

The Kansas City Star, April 29, 1997. p. 1. Burnes, Brian, and White, Tanika, "Garment District Companies Gone, but Memories are Revived."

New York Times, March 26, 1911, p. 1. "141 Men and Girls Die in Waist Factory Fire; Trapped High Up in Washington Place Building; Street Strewn with Bodies; Piles of Dead Inside."

Chicago Sunday Tribune, March 26, 1911, p. 1. "New York Fire Kills 148."

New York Times, March 26, 1911, p. 4. "Stories of Survivors. And Witnesses and Rescuers Outside Tell What They Saw."

New York Times, March 26, 1911, p. 4. "Crowd At Police Station; Mercer Street is Turned Into an Emergency Hospital"

New York Times, March 26, 1911, p. 4. "Death List Shows Few Identified"

Websites

http://www.ilr.cornell.edu/trianglefire/

http://history1900s.about.com/od/1910s/p/trianglefire.htm

http://www.csun.edu/~ghy7463/mw2.html

http://www.pbs.org/wgbh/americanexperience/films/triangle/player/

http://www.historybuff.com/library/refshirtwaist.html

http://law2.umkc.edu/faculty/projects/ftrials/triangle/triangleaccount.html

http://www.eyewitnesstohistory.com/snpim3.htm

http://www.womenscouncil.org/cd_web/Reed.html

http://www.umkc.edu/whmckc/PUBLICATIONS/MCP/MCPPDF/Worley-1-28-93.pdf

http://www.kcgarmentmuseum.org/

http://www.ameliaishmael.com/documents/critiquing/SDA_KCGM.pdf

http://cas.umkc.edu/labor-ed/history.htm

http://www.kclabor.org/garment_workers.htm

A sculpture near 8th and Broadway depicting a huge needle and button reminds the people of Kansas City of what once was.